THE WORLD'S GREATEST
HOTELS
RESORTS
+SPAS

Hanging out at Fabriken Furillen, in Sweden.

TRAVEL+ LEISURE

THE WORLD'S GREATEST
HOTELS RESORTS +SPAS

SIXTH EDITION

TRAVEL+ LEISURE BOOKS

AMERICAN EXPRESS PUBLISHING CORPORATION
NEW YORK

4

TRAVEL+LEISURE
THE WORLD'S GREATEST HOTELS, RESORTS + SPAS
SIXTH EDITION

Editors Irene Edwards, Jennifer Miranda
Consulting Editor Laura Begley Bloom
Art Director Wendy Scofield
Assistant Editor Kathryn O'Shea-Evans
Associate Managing Editor Laura Teusink
Photo Editor Beth Garrabrant
Production Associate Patrick Sheehan
Editorial Assistant Dorkys Ramos
Reporters Catesby Holmes, James Jung, Sarah Khan, Jane Margolies, Alison Miller, Bree Sposato, Sarah Storms, Laura Teusink, Meeghan Truelove
Copy Editors David Gunderson, Diego Hadis, Mike Iveson, Sarah Khan, Libby Sentz
Researchers Elena North-Kelly, Sonal Shah, Nate Storey

TRAVEL + LEISURE
Editor-in-Chief Nancy Novogrod
Creative Director Bernard Scharf
Executive Editor Jennifer Barr
Managing Editor Mike Fazioli
Arts/Research Editor Mario R. Mercado
Copy Chief Kathy Roberson
Photo Editor Whitney Lawson
Production Director Rosalie Abatemarco-Samat
Production Manager Ayad Sinawi

AMERICAN EXPRESS PUBLISHING CORPORATION
President and Chief Executive Officer Ed Kelly
Chief Marketing Officer and President, Digital Media
Mark V. Stanich
CFO, SVP, Corporate Development and Operations
Paul B. Francis
VP, General Managers Keith Strohmeier, Frank Bland
VP, Books and Products Marshall Corey
Director, Book Programs Bruce Spanier
Senior Marketing Manager, Branded Books
Eric Lucie
Assistant Marketing Manager Stacy Mallis
Director of Fulfillment and Premium Value
Philip Black
Manager of Customer Experience and Product
Development Charles Graver
Director of Finance Thomas Noonan
Associate Business Manager Uma Mahabir
Operations Director Anthony White

Cover: Qasr Al Sarab Desert Resort by Anantara

ISBN 978-1-932624-37-3 | ISSN 1559-0372
Published by American Express
Publishing Corporation
1120 Avenue of the Americas
New York, New York 10036

Distributed by Charlesbridge Publishing
85 Main Street, Watertown, Massachusetts 02472

Printed in Canada

A lobby sitting area in San Juan, Puerto Rico's Hotel SoFo CasaBlanca.

6

The lakeside terrace
and gardens at
Glenmere Mansion,
in Chester, New York.

contents

KEY TO THE PRICE ICONS $ UNDER $250 $$ $250–$499 $$$ $500–$749 $$$$ $750–$999 $$$$$ $1,000 AND UP

8

Dining at the Michelberger
Hotel, in Berlin.

KEY TO THE PRICE ICONS   **$** UNDER $250   **$$** $250–$499   **$$$** $500–$749   **$$$$** $750–$999   **$$$$$** $1,000 AND UP

A garden path leading
to guest rooms at
Hoshinoya Kyoto, in Japan.

KEY TO THE PRICE ICONS $ UNDER $250 $$ $250–$499 $$$ $500–$749 $$$$ $750–$999 $$$$$ $1,000 AND UP

A private daybed at Phulay Bay,
a Ritz-Carlton Reserve, in Krabi, Thailand.

introduction

ONCE AGAIN, WE'RE PROUD TO INTRODUCE T+L'S ANNUAL BOOK, *The World's Greatest Hotels, Resorts & Spas*, revealing our editors' selection of the year's most noteworthy properties. They all share a distinctive sense of arrival: you know right away that you've traded in the everyday for a new and different world, from the drama of Amangiri, built (literally) into the sandstone canyons of Utah, to the gleaming surfaces and sweeping skyline views of the Upper House, in Hong Kong.

Above all, the more than 650 hotels and resorts spotlighted in this book demonstrate that good design is about taking a more humanistic approach to interiors. As Glenn Pushelberg of Yabu Pushelberg, the firm that designed Mexico City's Las Alcobas—featured on pages 76–77—has said: "One should feel the natural beauty of the space, not just see the adornment." It's a fitting maxim for a property like the Shangri-La Hotel, Paris, set in a former palais that belonged to one of Napoleon Bonaparte's grandnephews. Comfortable and airy, the property manages to retain its scale and decorative details while introducing modern amenities.

Finding the authentic and the intimate is in fact the holy grail for our readers. Thus, Germany's Heidelberg Suites, in a 19th-century villa in Heidelberg's Old Town, will strike a chord. The Royal Mansour Marrakech, a cluster of 53 town houses with silk-paneled walls in the medina, could only be a product of that historic city, where timeless North African style is being reinterpreted through an intriguingly modern lens. Even the Armani Hotel Dubai, nestled into 10 floors of what is currently the world's tallest building, the Burj Khalifa, is authentic in its own way—think of it as Gulf State luxury to the max.

There's much more, of course: the re-creation of an early-20th-century garden by the renowned American landscape designer Beatrix Farrand at Glenmere Mansion, an imposing upstate New York manor that has been transformed into a welcoming country-house hotel. Or the strikingly modern Eco Beach Wilderness Retreat, in Broome, Australia, which is dedicated to preserving the region's rugged environment. Or the playful yet grown-up reinvention of Le Royal Monceau, Raffles Paris under Singapore-based Raffles Hotels & Resorts; designer Philippe Starck proves that he has lost none of his ability to surprise and enchant.

Not to be overlooked are two of our editorial mainstays, the World's Best Awards and the T+L 500, roundups of the top hotels as rated by our readers that you'll find beginning on page 218. Judging from the results of the World's Best Awards poll for the larger part of the past decade, visiting far-flung destinations—and deriving a high level of satisfaction from them—is a shared experience among our readers. That the three highest-ranking hotels in the most recent survey are, in descending order, Oberoi Vanyavilas, a jungle camp on the edge of India's Ranthambore tiger reserve; Triple Creek Ranch, in Darby, Montana, a haven for comfort-seeking outdoor-adventure travelers; and Fairmont Mara Safari Club, in Kenya's Masai Mara, speaks volumes. No doubt the distinctive encounters with the natural world afforded by these properties linger in memories treasured over a lifetime.

Finally, the back of this book includes a helpful resource section to help you navigate and search for properties by location and by category, from family-friendly to affordable. This will allow you to make the most of your adventures and to uncover the delights of travel—whether you're headed to new places or revisiting the ones you think you know. One thing is for sure: when you get there, you'll know you've definitely arrived.

NANCY NOVOGROD EDITOR-IN-CHIEF

The penthouse living room at
Glenmere Mansion, in New York.

united states & canada

WATCH HILL NEW YORK CITY CHESTER WASHINGTON, D.C. BEAUFORT BOCA G
LAMORADA MIAMI NEW ORLEANS MARFA TAOS CANYON POINT PARK CIT
AS VEGAS MANZANITA TRUCKEE LOS ANGELES KAUAI VANCOUVER TORON
ONTREAL WATCH HILL NEW YORK CITY CHESTER WASHINGTON, D.C. BEAUF
OCA GRANDE ISLAMORADA MIAMI NEW ORLEANS MARFA TAOS CANYON PO
TY LAS VEGAS MANZANITA TRUCKEE LOS ANGELES KAUAI VANCOUVER TOR
ONTREAL WATCH HILL NEW YORK CITY CHESTER WASHINGTON, D.C. BEA
OCA GRANDE ISLAMORADA MIAMI NEW ORLEANS MARFA TAOS SOUTHE

OCEAN HOUSE

Watch Hill, Rhode Island

ONCE THIS WAS THE QUINTESSENTIAL New England summer getaway: built in 1868 on a hill that peers out over the Atlantic, it catered to the boldfaced society names of the era. After years of neglect that rendered more than half its rooms unusable, the iconic seaside resort was torn down and painstakingly rebuilt with as many of its original details as possible. The sweeping porches and manicured croquet lawns are a return to old-world glamour, but the 49 light-drenched guest rooms and 22 private residences (six of which are available for rent) are much more spacious than those at the previous property. A 12,000-square-foot spa with organic products and five restaurants, including the farm-to-table-inspired Seasons, ensure the hotel is firmly rooted in the modern age. Stroll out to the 600-foot private beach, however, with its cabanas and cocktail pavilion, and the 21st century seems a distant memory. *1 Bluff Ave.; 888/552-2588; oceanhouseri.com; doubles from $$$.*

The view from the back deck at Ocean House, overlooking a private beach. Opposite: A patio near the resort's croquet field.

A living room sitting area in a suite at
Andaz Wall Street. Left: The chef's table
at the hotel's Wall & Water restaurant.

ANDAZ WALL STREET

New York City

THE STOCK MARKET HAS HAD its share of ups and downs, but at least one thing is bullish on Wall Street: the David Rockwell–
designed Andaz in the former Barclays Bank building. In lieu of a conventional check-in desk, a host greets you in the
lobby, offers you a seat and a glass of wine, then enters your name into a handheld PC to produce a key card on the spot.
Dark oak floors and oversize tubs add panache to the 253 guest rooms, as do the mini-bars stocked with complimentary
chips, chocolates, and nonalcoholic drinks. (Even more treats are on hand at the lobby's 24-hour free snack table.) A
locavore philosophy prevails at the hotel's restaurant, Wall & Water, which hosts cooking classes and a farmers' market from
May to November. Gordon Gekko types, however, may feel more at home at the slick Bar Seven Five, where a bartender
mixes Manhattans tableside from a pullman caddy.
75 Wall St.; 800/233-1234 or 212/590-1234; andaz.com; doubles from $$.

CROSBY STREET HOTEL

New York City

NO NEED FOR A TRIP across the pond to get a good dose of London chic. On a cobblestoned street in Manhattan's SoHo neighborhood, the Crosby Street Hotel is full of British design doyenne Kit Kemp's signature tongue-in-cheek flourishes, from the boldly patterned wing chairs in the drawing room to the portraits of local dogs in the elevators. The 86 rooms forsake chilly minimalism in favor of color, texture, and light, thanks to vibrant fabrics and floor-to-ceiling windows. Afternoon tea, complete with an assortment of tarts, scones, and sandwiches, is served all day, and on Sundays the hotel hosts dinner-and-a-movie nights in its private screening room. Still, it's the pitch-perfect service that will win you over: the umbrella at the ready for impending rain, the driver waiting to whisk you uptown to see the sights, or the proper hot toddy prepared with a smile at the bar. *79 Crosby St.; 800/553-6674 or 212/226-6400; firmdale.com; doubles from $$.*

Gazing down at SoHo from a Crosby Street Hotel guest room.

20

The forested acres surrounding the Glenmere Estate. Opposite, from top: The Supper Room; a marble-lined bathroom.

GLENMERE MANSION

Chester, New York

TURNING A SHUTTERED GILDED AGE ESTATE in a rural part of the Hudson Valley into a luxe 19-room hotel might seem a daunting proposition—particularly if the owners have zero experience as hoteliers and no one's ever heard of the location. But travelers in the know have been flocking to Glenmere since it opened in early 2010. Built a century ago on a hill overlooking a lake and 150 acres of meadows and woods, the pink Tuscan-style villa was rescued from decades of Miss Havisham–like disarray to the tune of $30 million. Guest rooms feature impeccably chosen modern art (a Robert Rauschenberg lithograph; a Robert Motherwell etching) and baths of Carrara marble. Downstairs, a main dining room serves prix fixe menus of regional ingredients, and terraces preside over formal beds of nepeta, roses, and boxwood. Best of all, the owners knew when to leave well enough alone: A walled garden originally designed by Beatrix Farrand, Edith Wharton's niece, remains an evocative ruin.

634 Pine Hill Rd.; 866/777-2992 or 845/469-1900; glenmere mansion.com; doubles from $$$, including breakfast.

W
WASHINGTON D.C.

Washington, D.C.

TWO BLOCKS FROM THE WHITE HOUSE, in a Beaux-Arts structure recently given a roguish revamp, the W seems adeptly suited for the next generation of Beltway insiders. In the high-ceilinged lobby, designer Dianna Wong kept the original chandeliers but retrofitted them with color-shifting LED lights and livened up a pin-striped sofa with throw pillows in black lace. Even more vivacious is the Point of View rooftop lounge, where red lacquered walls and 12-foot-tall windows form the backdrop for a menu of labor-intensive cocktails dreamed up by Sasha Petraske, New York City's master mixologist. Guest rooms are illuminated by backlit headboards and lamps fashioned from miniature busts of George Washington; suites take the aesthetic one step further, with digitally controlled fireplaces, violet leather chairs, and glossy white desks festooned with silver tassels. The final touch: expansive views that stretch from the Washington Monument to the Lincoln Memorial and the Pentagon. Talk about a power trip. *515 15th St. NW; 877/946-8357 or 202/661-2400; whotels.com; doubles from $$.*

The W Washington D.C.'s
statement-making lobby.

The wraparound veranda at Rhett House Inn. Opposite, from left: A Southern breakfast of eggs, grits, and biscuits; a Deluxe Inn room.

RHETT HOUSE INN

Beaufort, South Carolina

IT'S FORTUNATE THAT GENERAL SHERMAN'S TROOPS spared Beaufort during the infamous 1864 March to the Sea: the historic town is still lined with moss-covered oaks and pre–Civil War mansions. One of the loveliest is the Rhett House Inn, an 1820 white-columned structure with a two-story porch and a backyard cottage that served as one of the country's first African-American schools. Each of the 17 rooms exudes antebellum elegance, and Southern hospitality still reigns supreme—in addition to a full country breakfast with stone-ground grits, you'll be treated to evening hors d'oeuvres and house-made desserts served in the kitchen until 10 p.m. There's a fully stocked honor bar in the reception area, and picking a fresh lime off the tree to garnish your gin and tonic is highly encouraged. Tour the town on one of the inn's bikes, or curl up with a book in the pine-floored parlor, where a faded old photo pays homage to the house's historic past.
1009 Craven St.; 888/480-9530 or 843/524-9030; rhetthouseinn.com; doubles from $, including breakfast.

The beach at Gasparilla Inn.
Left: BZ's Terrace restaurant.

GASPARILLA INN & CLUB

Boca Grande, Florida

PICTURE AN EDENIC SLICE of Old Florida: whimsically named streets, an 1890 lighthouse, and long, quiet beaches lapped by gentle surf. That's the appeal of Boca Grande, a sleepy village on the Gulf of Mexico's Gasparilla Island, where tackle shops and funky seafood joints coexist with blue-blood enclaves. The Gasparilla Inn practically defines old guard—listed on the National Register of Historic Places, the Georgian-style 1913 resort has been a generations-old favorite of families bearing names like Rockefeller and du Pont. (Jeb and George H.W. Bush are winter-season regulars.) Interiors are tasteful and timeless, with plenty of floral-print fabrics and a stuffed tarpon or two. Dress for dinner in the main dining room, where jackets are required at the height of the season, and bring your regulation whites to play on the outdoor croquet field. The 18-hole Pete Dye–designed golf course is so exclusive that no tee times are necessary.
500 Palm Ave.; 877/403-0599 or 941/964-4500; gasparillainn.com; doubles from $$.

An idyllic spot along the shore at Moorings Village Resort. Right: An inviting bungalow veranda.

MOORINGS VILLAGE RESORT

Islamorada, Florida

EVEN THOUGH IT HAS SERVED AS THE BACKDROP for countless fashion-magazine photo shoots, this dreamy spread—18 brightly accented cottages connected by sand and wooden walkways on a former coconut plantation in the Florida Keys—still seems like your own secret discovery. Lush, almost jungle-like landscaping gives way to a private white-sand beach with swaying hammocks and a thatched-roof dock that convey barefoot luxury at its best. Bring back a few pounds of succulent stone-crab claws from the fish market to feast on in your room's kitchen, or head across the street to the Moorings' sister restaurant, Morada Bay Beach Café, for Bahamian-style conch fritters, coconut-crusted snapper, and a plethora of dangerously addictive rum cocktails. Kitsch alert: your drink shows up in an oversize Mason jar illuminated by a bobbing glow stick, all the better to toast the sunset.

123 Beach Rd.; 305/664-4708; mooringsvillage.com; cottages from $$.

TEMPO MIAMI,
A ROCKRESORT

Miami

A Deluxe Premium suite at Tempo
Miami. Opposite: The sky pool deck,
surrounded by Loft suites.

MIAMI HAS BEEN KNOWN AS A CITY OF larger than life hotels since the 1950's, but Tempo Miami is recasting the suntan capital's sometimes brash décor in a softer light. On the first 14 floors of a striking Arquitectonica-designed building downtown, located in a once dormant corridor along Biscayne Bay, the 70-room resort has expansive guest quarters (the smallest is 450 square feet), with understated palettes and floor-to-ceiling views of the cityscape or water. In keeping with the fitness-minded crowd, there's an 8,000-square-foot gym and spa next to the rooftop pool. At the restaurant, Amuse, small plates include scallop carpaccio with black olives, lemon oil, and lychees. The siren call of South Beach is just a 10-minute drive away, but there are even more immediate diversions at hand: first-rate opera, ballet, and symphony performances at the Adrienne Arscht Center for the Performing Arts across the street, and the Miami Heat stadium and future Miami Art Museum down the block.

1100 Biscayne Blvd.; 877/857-7625 or 786/369-0300; rockresorts.com; doubles from $.

spotlight *new orleans*

NEW ORLEANS IS AN ARTIST'S DREAM, surprising you with detail and beauty that unspools for blocks. Its recent history may be one of repair and recovery, but its architectural flow is a joyous ensemble visible in some of the city's best hotels. On the edge of the French Quarter, the boho-chic International House recently received a revamp from Los Angeles decorator to the stars L. M. Pagano, with rich fabrics and gilded textures that complement the Beaux-Arts building's decorative moldings and ornate pilasters. Don't miss the nightly ritual to welcome the spirits, held in the candlelit bar. One street south of the *Vieux Carré*, the historic Roosevelt (formerly the preferred hangout of Huey Long and Louis Armstrong) has undergone a $170

An L. M. Pagano chair in a Superior room at International House.

The Roosevelt New Orleans's restored façade.

INTERNATIONAL HOUSE

221 Camp St.; 800/633-5770 or 504/553-9550; ihhotel.com; doubles from $.

ROOSEVELT NEW ORLEANS, A WALDORF ASTORIA HOTEL

million renovation that includes a revitalized lobby, an Italian restaurant from native son John Besh, and a new Guerlain spa—one of only three in the country. Rising among the moss-shrouded oaks on St. Charles Avenue in the heart of the Garden District, the Columns Hotel has been restored to its original appearance, as it looked before Louis Malle filmed *Pretty Baby* there in 1978. The 1883 Italianate mansion remains a bona fide neighborhood haunt thanks to its Victorian Lounge—all smoke-burnished mahogany and creaking floorboards under a stained-glass chandelier. The property is a fitting addition to a city aptly dubbed Hollywood South: cinematic in its intermingling of the handsome, the ruined, and the sublime.

The veranda at the Columns Hotel.

123 Baronne St.; 800/925-3673 or 504/648-1200; therooseveltneworleans.com; doubles from $$.

COLUMNS HOTEL

3811 St. Charles Ave.; 800/455-9308 or 504/899-9308; thecolumns.com; doubles from $, including breakfast.

EL COSMICO

Marfa, Texas

LEAVE IT TO LIZ LAMBERT to make a trailer park chic. On an 18-acre plot in the art colony of Marfa, Texas, the idiosyncratic hotelier established the definitive retreat for desert bohemians: five refurbished trailers with mini kitchens, birch-veneer walls, and beds topped with Bolivian wool blankets. For those craving even less separation between themselves and the landscape, the property offers tent camping, yurts, and even a tepee stocked with a king-size futon. Solar-heated showers (some private) and a communal outdoor kitchen provide most of the comforts of home, while the occasional antelope grazes in the distance. In keeping with Marfa's creative spirit, El Cosmico regularly hosts music festivals and art workshops, and soon will feature a good old-fashioned darkroom—the better to capture wide-open West Texas panoramas straight out of a Coen Brothers production. *802 S. Highland Ave.; 877/822-1950 or 432/729-1950; elcosmico.com; doubles from $.*

Inside the 1951 Kozy Coach at El Cosmico. Opposite: The trailer at sunset.

BAVARIAN LODGE & RESTAURANT

Taos, New Mexico

AS A TRIBUTE TO HIS NATIVE BAVARIA, German entrepreneur Thomas Schulze re-created a traditional Alpine inn—log construction, lederhosen, and all—halfway up Taos Mountain, at an altitude of 10,200 feet. Schuss into the wood-beamed dining room to warm yourself by a traditional *Kachelofen* tile stove as dirndl-clad servers ply you with heaping platters of goulash, sauerbraten, and schnitzel. Once you're properly thawed and generously fed, retire to one of four individually decorated suites (the velvet-draped Lola Montez; the frescoed King Ludwig) or one of the recently opened three-bedroom chalets designed by interiors maven Alexandra Champalimaud. Stainless-steel fireplaces and industrial cabinetry are contemporary nods to Taos's mining past, while reproductions of 1950's ski posters and views of the towering pines along the Sangre de Cristo mountains hint at the black-diamond trails beyond.
100 Kachina Rd.; 888/205-8020 or 575/776-8020; thebavarian.net; doubles from $$.

AMANGIRI

Canyon Point, Utah

EVERY SURFACE OF AMANGIRI—the second North American property from luxury hotel group Amanresorts—seems to suggest not only an aesthetic but a meditative state of mind. Encircled by dramatic, dun-colored rock formations, the compound is set on 600 acres of southern Utah wilderness alongside eroded hoodoos and 5,000-year-old petroglyphs. Its polished, low-slung buildings, dyed up to 10 times to match the nuances of the landscape, house 34 streamlined suites with timber-and-rawhide furniture and smooth concrete walls that frame surreal sweeps of sculpted sandstone. Bathrooms are equipped with deep soaking tubs and rain showers, and the 25,000-square-foot spa has five treatment rooms plus a Flotation Pavilion (imagine a shallow saltwater pool within a cave). Come evening, after a dinner of roasted elk with cherry sauce, stargazing from a sky bed atop one of the pool suites ends the night on a high note. It's an instant classic for the less-is-more crowd. *1 Kayenta Rd.; 800/477-9180 or 435/675-3999; amanresorts.com; doubles from $$$$.*

A reflection pool at Amangiri's spa.
Opposite: The resort's austere exterior

WALDORF ASTORIA PARK CITY

Park City, Utah

DESPITE ITS SCALE, THE FIRST SKI PROPERTY from Waldorf Astoria is surprisingly intimate. Texture lends warmth to public spaces, from the mohair curtains behind the reception desk to the velvety panels that line the walls at the hotel's Spruce restaurant, one of Utah's best. But, as you would expect from the urbane chain, there are a few grand gestures as well, like the custom Baccarat chandelier that dominates the double-height lobby and the expansive hearth flanked by hand-carved wooden reindeer. Rooms, many with balconies, mountain views, and gas fireplaces, make an ideal base for couples, while the suites, with Viking-equipped kitchens and outdoor fire pits, serve as deluxe crash pads for the entire family. Hitting the slopes is as easy as hopping aboard the gondola across the street, and the après-ski rewards are plenty: a Mountain Salvation massage at the Golden Door Spa, followed by a hearty dinner of elk and potatoes.

2100 Frostwood Dr.; 800/925-3673 or 435/647-5500; waldorfastoria.com; doubles from $$$.

The pool area at the Waldorf Astoria
Park City. Opposite: Spruce restaurant.

A City Room at
Cosmopolitan Las Vegas.

COSMOPOLITAN LAS VEGAS

Las Vegas

FROM THE OUTSIDE, THE COSMOPOLITAN LOOKS LIKE any other glass-and-steel Vegas skyscraper. Inside, however, it's a different matter entirely. Video columns in the lobby are programmed with cutting-edge works of interactive art. Along one corridor of the sunlight-filled casino, walls are covered in hand-stitched chocolate leather. Factor in the artist-in-residence program's P3Studio, the edgy videos looping on the massive marquee, and the ground-level store from avant-garde Dutch company Droog, and it becomes clear that the 2,995-room property bears little resemblance to the status quo on the Strip. The roster of restaurants includes outposts from El Bulli protégé José Andrés, Italian chef Scott Conant, and Manhattan's Blue Ribbon Sushi. Even the smallest details are meticulously considered: the Fornasetti wallpaper lining the closets; the intricately carved sandstone walls in the desert-themed spa. This is the standard for Sin City's future.

3708 Las Vegas Blvd. S.; 877/551-7778 or 702/698-7000; cosmopolitanlasvegas.com; doubles from $, two-night minimum on weekends.

One of Coast Cabins'
cedar-shingled cottages.

COAST CABINS

Manzanita, Oregon

RAIN LASHES THE SURF, waves roar, and unruly patches of beach grass dot the landscape of this turbulent northern stretch of Oregon's shoreline. But if the coast is primeval, so too have been the hotel options—until recently. Twenty minutes south of Cannon Beach, in the windswept town of Manzanita, Coast Cabins evokes the woodsy charm of the Pacific Northwest, with five cedar-shingled cottages tucked into a Zen-like bamboo grove a few blocks from the shore. Each unit comes with feather beds, LCD TV's, free Wi-Fi, and private patios; most have Sub-Zero refrigerators, outdoor hot tubs, and fire pits hidden behind walls of dry-stacked rock and cedar. A sauna and a communal outdoor campfire space help ward off the brisk ocean air, as does the nightly s'mores ritual: kits of organic graham crackers, chocolate, and marshmallows are thoughtfully provided, but the stories are on you.

635 Laneda Ave.; 800/435-1269 or 503/368-7113; coastcabins.com; doubles from $.

CEDAR HOUSE SPORT HOTEL

Truckee, California

The lobby fireplace at
Cedar House Sport Hotel.

SURROUNDED BY 18 SKI RESORTS—the densest concentration of slopes anywhere in America—Lake Tahoe plays host to nearly every winter sport imaginable. But these days, it's the region's northern communities that are getting all the attention. Case in point: the historic town of Truckee, the setting for the Cedar House Sport Hotel. At once sleekly minimalist and appealingly rustic, the 42-room eco-lodge (which was inspired by ski villages in the Alps) was crafted from sustainably harvested woods and features a "living roof" over the reception area. Platform beds and bent-plywood furnishings add to the European air, and a concrete-and-steel fireplace in the lobby serves as a natural post-ski gathering spot. Owners Jeff and Patty Baird live on site and are happy to share their tips on the area's best hiking, biking, sailing, and skiing opportunities—such as the half-pipe at North America's only Burton Snowboard Academy, in nearby Northstar-at-Tahoe.
10918 Brockway Rd.; 866/582-5655 or 530/582-5655; cedarhousesporthotel.com; doubles from $, including breakfast.

The Butterfly Bar at Petit Ermitage. Opposite, from top: Surveying the saltwater pool; garden dining at the Private Rooftop Club.

PETIT ERMITAGE

Los Angeles

THE SUNSET STRIP IS ONLY a block away, but Petit Ermitage feels more akin to a private auberge in Paris—albeit one with an affordable price tag. Inside the 80-suite property, handwoven Turkish carpets and art by Dalí and de Kooning mix with Roman mosaic tiles and furnishings crafted from antique woods. Many guest rooms come with working fireplaces and updated kitchenettes. The highlight of the property (and a draw for such A-listers as Sienna Miller and Salma Hayek) is the rooftop club overlooking the Hollywood Hills, which features a saltwater pool, a hummingbird garden, and an outdoor movie screen where international films are shown every Sunday night. For the ultimate in privacy, book one of the 11 suites on the VIP fourth floor—you'll have a dedicated butler, aptly titled the Liaison to Happiness, tending to your every whim. *8822 Cynthia St.; 310/854-1114; petitermitage.com; doubles from $.*

The pool at the St. Regis
Princeville, overlooking Hanalei
Bay and Mount Makana.

ST. REGIS PRINCEVILLE RESORT

Kauai, Hawaii

FOR ITS FIRST HAWAIIAN PROPERTY, St. Regis took over a 25-year-old hotel with an impressive pedigree and a spectacular cliff-top location. After a multimillion-dollar renovation, the former Princeville Resort retains its longtime appeal with a few modern updates. The 252 rooms (some of Kauai's largest) make the most of their tropical setting with seashell colors and floor-to-ceiling windows that turn opaque at the flick of a switch. Chef Jean-Georges Vongerichten now helms the popular Kauai Grill, where ahi tuna comes with a rice-cracker crust and roasted foie gras is served with local longan fruit. Outside, the redesigned infinity pool fronts a sugar-sand beach protected by Puu Poa Reef, and the new spa offers guests signature treatments that are inspired by waterfalls and draw on plants sourced from the Hawaiian rain forest. Of course, one thing that hasn't changed is the hotel's staff of more than 450—some of whom are 25-year veterans of the property—which is rightfully considered to be the best on the island.
5520 Ka Haku Rd.; 888/627-7124 or 808/826-9644; princevillehotelhawaii.com; doubles from $$$$.

The Fairmont Pacific Rim's indoor-outdoor Chairman's Suite.

FAIRMONT PACIFIC RIM

Vancouver

WHEN SPECTATORS DESCENDED ON Vancouver for the 2010 Winter Olympics, the new Fairmont Pacific Rim was there just in time to greet them. Set along Coal Harbour, with views that sweep from Stanley Park to the North Shore Mountains, the sleek 800,000-square-foot property is one of the tallest buildings downtown. At check-in, you'll be serenaded by a pianist on a $225,000 white Fazioli grand (complete with 18-karat-gold hinges) before you're shown to your high-tech digs, where a bedside touch screen controls everything from the curtains to the temperature. Other in-room amenities include personal espresso machines and LCD TV's with surround sound; on the roof, an outdoor pool is flanked by private cabanas fit for the city's Hollywood North set on break from filming. Similarly, the hotel's BMW stands by for complimentary rides to any downtown location.

1038 Canada Place; 800/441-1414 or 604/695-5300; fairmont.com; doubles from $$.

A king Deluxe room, designed by Studio Gaia, at Thompson Toronto.

THOMPSON TORONTO

Toronto

THE FIRST FOREIGN OUTPOST of New York City's decidedly downtown hotel brand feels right at home in Toronto's artsy Central King West Village, with its neighboring fashion and financial districts. Don't mistake this for a quiet retreat—a cosmopolitan atmosphere rules, from the modelesque staff to the rooftop lounge and pool deck that reaches maximum capacity on weekend nights. In contrast, rooms are soothing and subdued, with chocolate-brown accents against crisp white Sferra bed linens. Amenities tend to be Manhattan-centric, including Dean & Deluca mini-bar snacks and bath products from C.O. Bigelow (not to mention the naughty boudoir items on sale from Kiki de Montparnasse). Another Big Apple import: the critically acclaimed Italian restaurant Scarpetta, from celebrity chef Scott Conant. But for those craving a cheeseburger in the middle of the night, Counter, the hotel's 24-hour haute diner, delivers the goods—along with (what else?) a classic *poutine*.

550 Wellington St. W.; 888/550-8368 or 416/640-7778; thompsonhotels.com; doubles from $.

LE PETIT HÔTEL

Montreal

CONTEMPORARY TOUCHES ARE ALL THE MORE COMPELLING in the context of a historic setting. Such is the case at Le Petit Hôtel, which has 24 rooms housed in two old buildings (including a 19th-century leather factory turned toy store) in the picturesque heart of Vieux-Montréal. Loftlike ceilings and rugged stone walls set off mod ergonomic furnishings tailored to young entrepreneurs; in the four "XL" rooms, the plasma TV's come outfitted with Wii Fit and Wii Sports. A black-and-white mural painted by local artists hangs in the bustling lobby café, which doubles as the reception area. Ask for a room at the back to avoid the street noise from passing revelers during late-night hours in summer—and wake up early for the complimentary continental breakfast, starring fresh and fluffy croissants from one of the city's incomparable *boulangeries*.

168 Rue St.-Paul Ouest; 877/530-0360 or 514/940-0360; petithotelmontreal.com; doubles from $, including breakfast.

A streetside view of Le Petit Hôtel. Opposite: The lobby café.

le petit

A Grand Luxury villa overlooking Petit Piton at Tides Sugar Beach, in St. Lucia.

caribbean
& the bahamas

CURAÇAO BEQUIA ST. LUCIA DOMINICA ST. KITTS TORTOLA SAN JUAN VIEQ
DOMINICAN REPUBLIC TURKS AND CAICOS HARBOUR ISLAND EXUMA CU
EQUIA ST. LUCIA DOMINICA ST. KITTS TORTOLA SAN JUAN VIEQUES DOMI
EPUBLIC TURKS AND CAICOS EXUMA HARBOUR ISLAND CURAÇAO BEQUI
DOMINICA ST. KITTS TORTOLA VIEQUES SAN JUAN DOMINICAN REPUBLIC
AICOS HARBOUR ISLAND EXUMA CURAÇAO BEQUIA ST. LUCIA DOMINICA
ORTOLA SAN JUAN VIEQUES DOMINICAN REPUBLIC TURKS AND CAICOS H

Snorkeling outside Avila Hotel's
Octagon wing.

AVILA HOTEL

Willemstad, Curaçao

IN TERMS OF CARIBBEAN GETAWAYS, the Avila represents the best of both worlds—it's minutes from downtown Willemstad, a UNESCO World Heritage site known for its quaint colonial buildings, and it's right on Curaçao's southern coast, where there are two small coves for swimming and snorkeling just a short walk away. (Serious divers know that the reefs just beyond the inlets are some of the best in the region for underwater exploring.) The former governor's mansion dates from the late 1700's; the loftlike guest rooms with spacious balconies in the Octagon wing are more recent additions. Owner Nic Møller, a music aficionado, regularly brings classical and jazz performers to the hotel's ballroom and on-site Blues Bar in the evening. The Avila even gets the royal stamp of approval: Queen Beatrix of the Netherlands stays here when she's on the island. No word, though, on whether she has succumbed to the temptations of the bar's Bon Bini cocktail, a mix of rum, pineapple and lemon juices, and Blue Curaçao, of course.
130 Penstraat; 800/747-8162 or 599-9/461-4377; avilahotel.com; doubles from $$.

Frangipani Hotel's laid-back exterior, as viewed from Admiralty Bay.

FRANGIPANI HOTEL

Bequia

THE EASYGOING FRANGIPANI REMAINS as hospitable and homey as it was 100 years ago, when it was built as a family residence by one of the island's preeminent sea captains. Located at the head of Admiralty Bay, steps from Port Elizabeth's ferry dock and lively downtown scene, the property consists of five simple guest rooms in a gingerbread-style main house and 10 upscale stone cottages with private bathrooms and balconies overlooking the water. "De Harbour," as the town is known, bustles with activity, particularly during the Easter Regatta, a favorite with yachtsmen from around the world. But Bequia's biggest party happens every Thursday night, when the Frangi hosts the spirited Jump Up. To the music of a steel-drum band, revelers feast on such West Indian specialties as breadfruit salad and salt-fish *buljol* and take the dancing out to the sand.

Admiralty Bay; 784/458-3255; frangipanibequia.com; doubles from $.

spotlight st. lucia

THE LUSH VOLCANIC ISLAND OF ST. LUCIA is an undersize, underexposed destination with outsize potential. The former British territory encompasses a staggering variety of landscapes, from jungle-draped peaks to black-sand beaches; luxurious marinas to sleepy Creole villages. Now a visionary plan for development is taking this relatively unsung gem to the next level, coupled with a crop of intimately scaled hotels that emphasize the island's culture and natural bounty. The staff at the Mediterranean-style Cap Maison, built into a cliff on the northern coast, takes guests on nature walks through farms and countryside, where cashew nuts, citrus, breadfruit, and bananas grow in abundance. Back to the land is also the theme at Fond Doux Holiday

The rooftop terrace of an ocean-view villa suite at Cap Maison.

Omowale Hippolyte, a tour guide at the Fond Doux Holiday Plantation.

CAP MAISON

Smugglers Cove Dr., Cap Estate, Gros Islet; 888/765-4985 or 758/457-8678; capmaison.com; doubles from $$, including breakfast.

FOND DOUX HOLIDAY PLANTATION

Etangs, Soufrière; 758/459-7545; fonddouxestate.com; doubles from $, including breakfast.

Plantation, a working farm and eco-resort owned and run by St. Lucians on the hills above Soufrière. Relaunching this fall as the first Caribbean-island Tides resort from Los Angeles–based Viceroy Group, Tides Sugar Beach, in the former Jalousie Plantation, will feature redone villas with a bird's-eye perch over the Val des Pitons. Farther south, on a former sugarcane plantation that dates from the 18th century, Balenbouche Estate consists of four lovingly decorated cottages rented out by the Lawaetz family. Be sure to visit the on-site jewelry workshop of younger daughter Anitanja—her eye-catching pieces, incorporating seeds, shells, and stones, are evocative mementos of the island's unique beauty.

White-sand shores at Tides Sugar Beach.

The historic plantation house at Balenbouche Estate.

TIDES SUGAR BEACH

Val des Pitons, Soufrière; 800/235-4300 or 758/456-8000; thejalousieplantation.com; villas from $$$$.

BALENBOUCHE ESTATE

Choiseul; 758/455-1244; balenbouche.com; doubles from $, three-night minimum.

CALIBISHIE COVE

Calibishie, Dominica

LOCATED ON THE MOUNTAINOUS ISLE'S northeastern corner, diminutive Calibishie Cove has simplicity down to an art. Think *effortless* in every sense of the word: all four whitewashed rooms have platform beds, large shutters that open to the breeze, and private patios that look out on the Caribbean Sea. Fresh-roasted Dominican coffee, handmade soaps, and snorkeling equipment are included in your stay; TV's aren't. But who would want them? This is the land of turquoise waterfalls, where you can swim among sea horses and turtles in the warm sea off near-empty Hodges Beach. Follow one of the hotel's guides on an early-morning hike to the Syndicate nature reserve—endangered Sisserou parrots nest within the rain-forest canopy. Or arrange for a picnic lunch of spiny lobster and head for the uninhabited shores of Treasure Island, a 10-minute kayak trip away.
Point Dubique; 443/987-6742; calibishiecove.com; doubles from $.

Calibishie Cove's Paradise Penthouse Suite.

The view of Dieppe Bay from a great-house patio at Golden Lemon Inn. Left: A beachfront villa.

GOLDEN LEMON INN & VILLAS

Dieppe Bay, St. Kitts

WHEN IT OPENED IN A VERDANT GARDEN on the black-sand banks of Dieppe Bay in 1963, the Golden Lemon was one of the Caribbean's first boutique hotels. It's still a little treasure with tons of personality, thanks to antiques-filled rooms (hand-carved four-poster beds; mahogany sideboards turned bathroom vanities) and an excellent West Indian restaurant serving rum-braised beef stew. The seven rooms in the 17th-century great house are charming, but the villas are the ones to book, with their 25-foot-high ceilings, sunken baths, and private plunge pools. The background noise is of the bucolic sort: yellow warblers chirping from the property's almond trees and the ocean breaking gently against the beach. Ask the owners to arrange a guided tour of the ruins of nearby sugar mills, or spend the afternoon snorkeling at Frigate Bay. Come evening, kick back on the veranda for cocktails with the other guests, many of whom discovered the Lemon years ago and have been coming back ever since.

Dieppe Bay; 869/465-7260; goldenlemon.com; doubles from $$.

Long Bay Beach Resort's palm-lined coast.

LONG BAY BEACH RESORT & VILLAS

Tortola, British Virgin Islands

SPRAWLED ACROSS 52 LEAFY ACRES on Tortola's western shore, Long Bay's low-slung, pastel-colored buildings cascade down a secluded hillside fronting a private white-sand beach. The 157 rooms range from rustic cabanas on stilts to two- or three-bedroom vacation houses with pools; all have wicker furnishings and ocean views. The largest of the British Virgin Islands, Tortola excels in underwater activities—the dive shop staff can arrange trips to sites like Rhone National Marine Park's coral-encrusted tunnels and a shipwrecked 19th-century pirate vessel teeming with kaleidoscopic sea life. Charter a sloop and sail to uninhabited Norman Island, said to be the inspiration for Robert Louis Stevenson's *Treasure Island* (and the backdrop for the 1950's film of the same name). But to truly embrace Tortola's "limin'" (chilled-out) atmosphere, book a kombu-and-sea-clay body wrap at the hotel spa, then order a papaya daiquiri at the swim-up bar. That's the isle of Jost Van Dyke glimmering like a jewel in the distance.

Road Town, Tortola; 800/345-0356 or 284/495-4252; longbay.com; doubles from $.

Hotel SoFo CasaBlanca's lobby. Opposite, from top: The modest exterior; bold accents in the reception area.

HOTEL SOFO CASABLANCA

San Juan, Puerto Rico

OLD SAN JUAN'S BURGEONING SOFO AREA—a once-neglected section of Calle Fortaleza—is now the city's go-to spot. Centuries-old soft-hued buildings have been converted into Nuevo Latino restaurants and moody, low-lit lounges popular with a young and glamorous crowd. Hotel SoFo CasaBlanca, a two-year-old addition on the buzziest part of the strip, has slipped gracefully into the scene, its 30 rooms decorated with Moroccan lanterns, mirrored Afghani bedspreads, and hand-glazed ceramic sinks. Public spaces are made for relaxing, either on the settees and daybeds in the lobby (which is lined with paintings by Puerto Rican artist Carlos Mercado) or in one of five stone plunge pools on the tranquil rooftop deck. Prefer a livelier backdrop? The nighttime festivities heat up around midnight at the Nuyorican Café, a space for live salsa and Latin-inflected jazz just steps from the hotel.
316 Calle Fortaleza; 787/725-3436; hotelcasablancapr.com; doubles from $.

The eclectic Living Room at the new W Retreat on Vieques.

W RETREAT & SPA, VIEQUES ISLAND

Vieques, Puerto Rico

THE SLEEPY ISLAND of Vieques, eight miles off Puerto Rico's southeastern coast, has become a prime destination for in-the-know travelers, but W Hotels' first Caribbean foray and its first Retreat property in North America raises the bar for stylish accommodations. Milan-based Spanish designer Patricia Urquiola transformed a former Wyndham into a modern haven, where the aesthetic is playful yet sophisticated and the spirit of indoor/outdoor living is in full effect. Splashy prints and rainbow-tinged woven loungers add punch to guest rooms and the Living Room, a social hub of a lobby that extends to an outdoor terrace with a fire pit and ocean views. VIP's can take the fun to one of the bi-level infinity pool's private cabanas, complete with refrigerators and plasma TV's.

Km 3.2, State Rd. 200; 877/946-8357 or 787/741-4100; whotels.com; doubles from $$$.

A treetop view of the Atlantic from
Hotel La Catalina's restaurant.

HOTEL LA CATALINA

Cabrera, Dominican Republic

SET IN A TROPICAL GARDEN ON A HILL OVERLOOKING the fishing town of Cabrera, Hotel La Catalina is better suited for peace-seekers than nightlife lovers. The family-owned inn was established as an intimate, friendly antidote to the Dominican Republic's behemoth all-inclusives, and still seems to exist in a bubble of tranquillity, 40 miles west of the tourist-trammeled beaches of Cabarete. Most of the 32 suites and condos have kitchenettes and private bougainvillea-framed balconies with ocean views. Go for a dip in one of the two pools, or hike to the nearby waterfall El Saltadero to cool off in the swimming hole (take the plunge from the cliffs above, if you dare). Want to find your own palm-fringed swath of sand? Some of the country's best—Caleton, Diamante, La Entrada, Orchid Bay, Playa Grande—are a short drive away.
Cabrera; 809/589-7700; lacatalina.com; doubles from $, including breakfast.

GANSEVOORT TURKS & CAICOS

Providenciales, Turks and Caicos

THE VIBE IS SOUTH BEACH MOD at this happening getaway along Grace Bay Beach. Guests recline on extra-wide chaise longues or on one of the "floating islands" that punctuate the 7,000-square-foot infinity pool, as Caribbean-inspired lounge music wafts in the background. Low-slung platform beds and glass-walled showers built for two keep things crisp and understated in the 91 rooms, and the staff looks just as sharp, thanks to tailored uniforms by Lacoste. Come nightfall, a well-dressed crowd bedecked in Diane von Furstenberg and Michael Kors flocks to the outdoor bar at Bagatelle Bistrot. Blink and you'd think you were at Bagatelle's sister restaurant, located near the Gansevoort in New York City's trendy Meatpacking District. *Grace Bay Beach; 888/844-5986 or 649/941-7555; gansevoortturksandcaicos.com; doubles from $$$.*

**Gansevoort Turks & Caicos's
pool and open-air lobby.
Opposite: Grace Bay Beach.**

Room 10 at Ocean View Club.
Opposite: Owner Pip
Simmons's son Will and
breakfast chef Ivy Cleare.

OCEAN VIEW CLUB

Harbour Island, Bahamas

ON CHEERY HARBOUR ISLAND, OFF THE TIP OF ELEUTHERA, cicadas rattle like castanets in the noonday heat and white picket fences front cottages painted baby pink and aquamarine. One such structure, the nine-room Ocean View Club, has been owned for the past four decades by Pip Simmons, a graduate of Paris's Le Cordon Bleu cooking school and a local style authority often credited with putting Harbour Island on the map. (Fans of the hotel have included the photographer Bruce Weber and Irish milliner to the stars Philip Treacy.) The feel is one of an intimate house party, in which familiar guests mingle at the bar before dinner and meander about the main house and three neighboring bungalows afterward, cocktails in hand. Paintings by the late Bahamian artist Amos Ferguson and a palette that ranges from parrot green to periwinkle ensure that interiors are fresh and distinctive. The surroundings aren't too shabby, either: right beyond your bedroom door lies Pink Sand Beach, a three-mile stretch of surf that's considered one of the best in the Bahamas. *Gaol Lane; 242/333-2276; oceanviewclub.com; doubles from $$.*

FOWL CAY RESORT

Exuma, Bahamas

CONSIDER THIS 50-ACRE PRIVATE ISLAND your own Caribbean cay—an exclusive, underpopulated paradise where you have as much or as little contact with the staff as you like. The six expansive villas (each with a stone patio, white rockers shaded by palmettos, and an oversize kitchen where your breakfast is cooked to order) sit on stilts above the rocky shoreline, where it's possible to stake out your own cove for a day of lazy relaxation. If adventure is your thing, an array of watersports equipment is at your disposal, from kayaks to Sunfish sailboats. Two deserted beaches front a sea packed with starfish and sand dollars; book a guided trip to neighboring waters to swim amid spotted eagle rays and subterranean stalagmites. Drying out in a rope hammock strung between two coconut palms, you'll feel as if you're the only person in the world.
888/487-6925 or 242/357-0095; royalplantationisland.com; villas from $$$$$ per couple, including meals, three-night minimum.

The living room at Birdcage House at Fowl Cay Resort. Opposite: The walkway at Starlight House, overlooking the Caribbean Sea.

La Nao restaurant at Banyan Tree Cabo Marqués.

mexico & central & south america

BAJA CALIFORNIA MEXICO CITY PLAYA XPU-HA ACAPULCO AMBERGRIS CAY
PUERTO VIEJO CARTAGENA COLCA CANYON LAKE TITICACA SANTIAGO
CORONEL BRANDSEN BUENOS AIRES JOSE IGNACIO JERICOACOARA BAJA
CALIFORNIA MEXICO CITY PLAYA XPU-HA ACAPULCO AMBERGRIS CAY PUE
VIEJO CARTAGENA COLCA CANYON LAKE TITICACA SANTIAGO CORONEL
BRANDSEN BUENOS AIRES JOSE IGNACIO JERICOACOARA BAJA CALIFORNI
MEXICO CITY PLAYA XPU-HA ACAPULCO AMBERGRIS CAY PUERTO VIEJO
CARTAGENA COLCA CANYON LAKE TITICACA SANTIAGO CORONEL BRAND

spotlight
baja california, mexico

NINETY MINUTES SOUTH OF SAN DIEGO, Ensenada and the nearby Valle de Guadalupe are increasingly known for their burgeoning wine scene and local bounty—huarache oysters, sweet baby abalone, ruby-red bluefin tuna. But this corner of Baja California is also the setting for a bevy of stylish new boutique hotels. Just outside the rough-and-ready port town of Ensenada, the nine-room Casa Natalie Hotel Boutique is a mellow bastion of sophistication, with natural stone and wood floors and handmade clay *chimeneas*. The handsome infinity pool and an open-air bar look out over a rocky beach and the silver-blue Pacific. Northeast along the winery-lined Ruta del Vino, La Villa del Valle occupies a two-story hilltop hacienda with 360-degree views. British owners Phil and Eileen Gregory have imbued the country inn with thoughtful touches, including bedside bottles of mint-infused water and sprigs of lavender on pillows. Nearby, the 12-room Hacienda Guadalupe is another husband-and-wife-run labor of love: Daniel Sanchez plays concierge, arranging hikes and trail rides, while Gabriela Sanchez cooks up eclectic creations using sustainable local ingredients, served with the property's own wines. At the sprawling Adobe Guadalupe—where the tiled-roof main building has rounded archways and a Roman-style cupola—six guest rooms, all named after archangels, open onto an arcaded courtyard with a fountain that provides the only sound you'll hear at night.

Casa Natalie Hotel Boutique's infinity pool, overlooking the Pacific Ocean.

The main living room at Adobe Guadalupe.

A living room at La Villa del Valle.

CASA NATALIE HOTEL BOUTIQUE

Km 103.3, Hwy. 1, El Sauzal de Rodríguez, Ensenada; 800/381-3568 or 52-646/174-7373; casanatalie.com; doubles from $$, including breakfast.

LA VILLA DEL VALLE

Rancho San Marcos, Valle de Guadalupe; 818/207-7130 or 52-646/156-8007; lavilladelvalle.com; doubles from $, including breakfast and an evening aperitif and canapé.

HACIENDA GUADALUPE

Km 81.5, Crta. Tecate-Ensenada, Valle de Guadalupe; 52-646/155-2860; haciendaguadalupehotel.com; doubles from $.

ADOBE GUADALUPE

Col. Rusa de Guadalupe, Valle de Guadalupe; 52-646/155-2094; adobeguadalupe.com; doubles from $, including breakfast and a wine tasting.

Hacienda Guadalupe's palm-fringed sauna and pool area.

The living room in Las Alcobas's
Pasaje Penthouse suite.

LAS ALCOBAS

Mexico City

CREATING AN INTIMATE ESCAPE in the heart of the buzzing Polanco district is no easy task. But that's exactly what design duo Yabu Pushelberg did with Las Alcobas, a 35-room refuge where soundproof walls and an earthy palette create a cocooning effect on busy Avenida Presidente Masaryk. The rosewood spiral staircase in the lobby is made for a movie-star entrance, a more than subtle indication of the service on hand: Each room is assigned a dedicated host who doubles as a personal concierge and butler, booking last-minute dinner reservations or drawing a warm bath with scented oils. Indigenous ingredients, including aloe vera, agave, and maize, are featured at the small but exquisite spa. And at the two restaurants, both helmed by acclaimed Mexico City chef Martha Ortiz, traditional dishes such as quesadillas with zucchini blossoms and duck in *mole negro* are accompanied by artisan-crafted mezcals and tequilas.

390 Avda. Presidente Masaryk; 52-55/3300-3900; lasalcobas. com; doubles from $$.

ESENCIA ESTATE

Playa Xpu-Ha, Mexico

CAN A YUCATÁN BEACH RESORT HELP SUSTAIN THE MAYAN WAY OF LIFE? That's the mission of preservation-minded Esencia, just half a mile from the giant resorts that line the Riviera Maya. Seventy-five percent of the staff members come from surrounding villages, and they helped design many of the property's features—including the *chucum*-walled spa, which was built using traditional construction methods. The guiding light is Doña Bena Tun, a local *mujer sabia*, or wise woman, who shares her knowledge of indigenous folklore, Mayan cuisine, and ancient herbs and rituals used for spa treatments. Elements of the jungle are integrated into the landscape, including the *ramones* ("trees of good vibrations") that line the paths; inside, many rooms have native hardwood furnishings that enhance the natural aesthetic. In this era of eco rhetoric, in which any resort can install a solar panel and tout its environmental sensitivity, Esencia is a place with both style and substance.
Crta. Cancún Tulum; 877/528-3490 or 52-984/873-4835; hotelesencia.com; doubles from $$$, including breakfast.

Esencia Estate's Sal y Fuego restaurant. Opposite: A bowl of indigenous cacao nuts.

Suites along the Pacific coast at Banyan Tree Cabo Marqués. Opposite, from top: A sofa in the reception area; lounge-style seating.

BANYAN TREE CABO MARQUÉS

Acapulco, Mexico

ONCE A PLAYGROUND FOR THE 1950'S Hollywood elite, the resort town of Acapulco is making a bid to recapture its former glory. Case in point: The new Banyan Tree Cabo Marqués. These are, quite simply, the region's most awe-inspiring guest rooms: glass-walled villas are suspended on stilts and staggered along the cliffs for privacy, with steeply pitched roofs and infinity-edge plunge pools on verandas designed to maximize views. Of course, the timber deck and overwater lounge boast impressive vistas of their own. Inside, the brand's impeccable Asian design blends streamlined pieces with artisanal Mexican details (honey-colored onyx lamps; talavera earthenware; handwoven textiles from Oaxaca), and the service is just as appealing. Attentive staffers are available to whisk guests from their villas to the holistic spa—try the Royal Banyan Herbal Pouch Massage using warm sesame oil—or to Saffron, the resort's signature Thai restaurant, whose chefs hail from another place the hotel group calls home: Phuket.

Lote 1, Blvd. Cabo Marqués, Colonia Punta Diamante; 800/591-0439 or 52-744/434-0100; banyantree.com; doubles from $$$.

The pool terrace at Hotel Boca
Chica Acapulco. Opposite:
Streamlined metal room
directionals on a hallway wall.

HOTEL BOCA CHICA ACAPULCO

Acapulco, Mexico

THE LATEST FROM DESIGN-FORWARD MEXICAN boutique chain Grupo Habita is the Midcentury Modern oceanfront Hotel Boca Chica Acapulco, whose iconic sign you might recognize from the 1963 Elvis film *Fun in Acapulco*. After a smart revamp, the property manages to look both appealingly retro and strikingly contemporary. Each of the 36 rooms has a white palette—except for a few pops of color—and jalousie doors that open onto a quiet terrace; most have water views. The signature brick latticework remains an exterior focal point, and the amoeba-shaped pool is ideally positioned for panoramas of the ecological preserve across the water. In the morning, sit down to *chilaquiles* under the restaurant's open-air *palapa*, end your night lounging on the terrace with an Acabrown, the hotel's addictive tamarind-and-mezcal cocktail.
Playa Caletilla; 800/337-4685 or 52-744/482-7879; hotel-bocachica.com; doubles from $.

XANADU ISLAND RESORT

Ambergris Cay, Belize

THIS IS THE PLACE YOU DREAM OF ON A BLUSTERY WINTER DAY: a warm-weather escape on an island with only three main streets (Front, Middle, and Back, as they're commonly known). Just outside the town of San Pedro and near the tip of 36-mile-long Ambergris Cay, the six thatched-roof casitas of Xanadu Island Resort encircle a pool flanked by coconut palms; a wooden boardwalk leads to the sand. The one-, two-, and three-bedroom units are spacious and comfortably furnished—they're a great choice for traveling families—and come with full kitchens and balconies that look out onto the gardens or the Caribbean Sea. You might arrive planning to spend your trip stretched out on the beach after you've fixed yourself a drink in your suite. But then you'd be missing Belize's famously exhilarating adventure options: a snorkeling excursion on the second-largest barrier reef in the world, or a 15-minute scenic flight to the mainland to climb up Mayan ruins and float in an inner tube through a cave lit only by your headlamp.

Beachfront, San Pedro; 011-501/226-2814; xanaduresort-belize.com; doubles from $, three-night minimum.

A *palapa* at Xanadu Island
Resort's pool area.
Opposite: Sitting on a rock
ledge overlooking the
Caribbean Sea.

Bright accents in a whitewashed
Deluxe room at Le Caméléon.

LE CAMÉLÉON

Puerto Viejo, Costa Rica

TRAVELERS WHO MAKE THE FOUR-HOUR JOURNEY from the capital of San José to this wild stretch of Caribbean coastline—a part of the country once known mainly to intrepid surfers for its waves—would do well to rent a vehicle with four-wheel drive. Your efforts will be rewarded upon check-in at the boutique hotel Le Caméléon, a bold addition to the laid-back scene. Twenty-three tranquil white rooms in a manicured rain-forest garden have iPod docking stations, mini-bars, and private outdoor terraces or balconies. At the open-air restaurant, Numu, the menu is Central American fusion (try the grilled sea bass with mashed yuca and leeks), and the tiki-torch-lit setting lends romantic ambience in the evenings. Days may be spent beach hopping: Golden Cocles Beach is right in front of the hotel, with even-quieter Playa Chiquita and Punta Uva less than an hour away.

Playa Cocles, Puerto Viejo Limón; 506/2750-0501; lecameleon hotel.com; doubles from $$, including breakfast.

Tcherassi Hotel's Ziberline suite. Left: The rooftop pool and lounge.

TCHERASSI HOTEL & SPA

Cartagena, Colombia

FOR THE PAST FEW YEARS, CARTAGENA HAS BEEN one of the most in-demand destinations in South America for sophisticated global travelers, and the Tcherassi is clearly meant for them. In the colonial walled Old City, the hotel was created by Colombian fashion designer Silvia Tcherassi, who converted a 250-year-old mansion into seven guest rooms that she named after luxurious fabrics. The white-on-white interiors of the Organdie, Mousseline, and Peau de Soie suites, among others, pop with funky decorative accents (tasseled bedspreads; "chandeliers" of interlocking plastic rings) reminiscent of the tactile accessories in her collections. Start your day with a five-course breakfast that includes fresh fruit, chorizo, and *carimañolas* (stuffed yuca fritters) in the courtyard, adjacent to a small-scale swimming pool and a three-story vertical garden. For dinner at the restaurant Vera, with its salvaged wood beams and backlit mirrors, the menu is inspired by coastal Italian dishes, courtesy of Daniel Castaño, a former protégé of Mario Batali.

6-21 Calle del Sargento Mayor; 877/575-2799 or 57-5/664-4445; tcherassihotels.com; doubles from $$, including breakfast.

A panoramic view of Las Casitas del Colca and the surrounding Colca Valley.

LAS CASITAS DEL COLCA

Colca Canyon, Peru

IN THE DEEPEST CANYON IN THE AMERICAS, a four-hour drive from Arequipa (Peru's second-largest city), the hidden paradise of Colca is rapidly becoming one of the continent's must-see spots. With this in mind, the Orient-Express hotel group expanded and refined a rustic seven-room lodge, turning it into the polished Las Casitas del Colca. Twenty additional cottages have private patios and heated plunge pools and are set on grounds that include ponds, stables, and a small lawn where baby alpacas are bottle-fed by staff and guests. At turndown, a sheepskin-encased hot-water bottle is left peeking from behind a pillow and candles ring the bathtub. Field guides with pop-up maps of the region are handed out at check-in, as is zinc-oxide sunblock—a necessity at 10,700 feet. Set out for condor-spotting or a trip to a pre-Incan village, followed by a massage with plant-infused oils beneath giant eucalyptus trees. It's the Andean outback, done in style.
Parque Curiña, Yanque; 800/237-1236 or 51-1/610-8300; lascasitasdelcolca.com; doubles from $$$, including meals and transportation from Arequipa.

TITILAKA

Lake Titicaca, Peru

ON A PENINSULA OVERLOOKING 3,205-square-mile Lake Titicaca, this landmark eco-lodge sets the bar high for responsible luxury. Its mission is to connect guests not only with the immediate environment—this is the world's highest navigable lake, backed by snowcapped mountains and the Andean altiplano—but also with the region's Aymara and Quechua people and traditions. Neighboring farmers supply the fish, alpaca meat, potatoes, and grains served at the window-lined restaurant; guided itineraries include excursions to village fiestas and ancient archaeological sites, as well as boat trips to the nearby islands of Uros and Taquile. With so much outdoor visual stimulation to contend with, interiors are restrained, though most have oversize soaking tubs, plus radiant-heat floors and blackout curtains to block the dazzling early-morning sunshine reflecting off the water.

Puno; 866/628-1777 or 51-1/700-5105; titilaka.com; doubles from $$$, all-inclusive.

Titilaka's brick exterior. Opposite, from left: A wooden walkway at the entrance; the lodge's gift shop.

A street view of the Aubrey.

THE AUBREY

Santiago, Chile

WHEN DOMINGO DURÁN MORALES, a prominent 20th-century politician and railroad tycoon, built his family residence at the entrance to Santiago's mountainous Parque Metropolitano, he probably never imagined it would become the city's most singular boutique hotel. Yet after a three-year renovation that incorporated an Art Deco mansion next door, the 1927 Tudor Revival house more than fits that description. In the dining room, where lawmakers once debated policy at weekly power meals, guests linger over leisurely dinners of hand-cut pappardelle pasta and local wines. A handsome carved-wood staircase connects the living areas to 11 contemporary suites (four more are in another wing), which have plaza-sized beds and balconies overlooking the leafy Bellavista neighborhood. Don't miss a visit to the former residence of Nobel Prize–winning poet Pablo Neruda, just around the corner.
317 Constitución; 56-2/940-2800; theaubrey.com; doubles from $, including breakfast.

FINCA MARÍA CRISTINA

Coronel Brandsen, Argentina

SIXTY MILES FROM BUENOS AIRES, the 55-acre Finca María Cristina evokes the romance of the Pampas—fertile, wide-open plains intrinsically linked in the Argentine imagination with gaucho culture. Like the landscape that surrounds them, the estancia's 20 rooms are simple and soothing, with blond wood floors and private decks; windows reach up to cathedral ceilings to let in plenty of sunlight; and roaring fires are lit at dusk to ward off the briskness of the country air. Outside, a circular pool occupies a tranquil space beneath a cluster of eucalyptus trees. The restaurant turns out artisanal pizzas in hive-shaped outdoor ovens, and the requisite *asado,* or barbecue, is a lip-smacking affair that would satisfy the hungriest cowboy. The best part? The hotel's helicopter can shuttle guests straight from the capital city in a mere 20 minutes. *Km 67.5, Ruta 215, Brandsen; 54-11/5279-4737; fincamaria cristina.com.ar; doubles from $, including meals.*

The porch at Finca María Cristina.
Below: Chaise longues by the pool.

Algodon Mansion's French-style entrance.

ALGODON MANSION

Buenos Aires

SET IN A BELLE ÉPOQUE TOWN HOUSE IN THE CHIC RECOLETA DISTRICT, the 10-suite Algodon Mansion feels more like a well-heeled Porteño's private residence—albeit one with a two-story waterfall in the foyer. Its owners spared no expense, installing fireplaces in several guest rooms, book-matched Italian *calacatta* marble bathrooms, and lapacho floors throughout. Under a gold-leafed ceiling in the hotel restaurant, chef Antonio Soriano serves a seasonal menu of dishes, such as grass-fed lamb chops with Andean potatoes or Patagonian black sea bass with black-olive gnocchi. You'll find top-notch cigars and a selection of premium cognacs in the adjacent cocktail lounge. On the roof, there's a spa and a pretty pool surrounded by teak decking and lounge seating. The urban aerie is also the perfect spot for a twilight tango—ask your 24-hour butler to arrange private lessons, followed by globally inspired drinks at the hotel's Sky Bar.
1647 Montevideo; 54-11/3530-7777; algodonmansion.com; doubles from $$$.

The pool and lounge at Arbol Casa Loft.

ARBOL CASA LOFT

José Ignacio, Uruguay

A TINY BEACH TOWN ON URUGUAY'S SOUTHERN COAST, José Ignacio has been tapped by the global cognoscenti as the next Punta del Este. But despite the long-limbed crowd with a penchant for partying, this community of low-lying buildings and natural bays has managed to retain its relaxed vibe. Near the main square, the six-room Arbol Casa Loft is set in tropical gardens dotted with sculptures by Argentine artist Juan Pintabona. Each room, done in soothing ivory tones and furnished with pieces from Indonesia, Malaysia, and Uruguay, opens onto an oceanfront balcony or shaded gravel terrace. Savor a simple breakfast of croissants and *dulce de leche* on a futon-like wooden beach lounge by the pool before making your way to white-sand Playa Brava nearby, with its surfer-worthy waves, or the more tranquil Playa La Mansa, a short walk from the hotel.
Los Teros; 54-11/4803-1113; arbolcasaloft.com; doubles from $$.

The swim-up pool bar at Chili Beach.

CHILI BEACH
BOUTIQUE HOTELS & RESORTS

Jericoacoara, Brazil

WITH ITS FRESHWATER LAGOONS AND SURREAL SAND DUNES, UNSPOILED JERICOACOARA is the background for Chili Beach, a compound of all-white suites and casitas. The rustic fishing village—there are no paved roads, and the town was wired for electricity only 13 years ago—is a five-hour drive from the nearest big city, Fortaleza; nonetheless, it has become a popular vacation landing place for bohemian jet-setters seeking a destination fit for a modern castaway. Although the surroundings are simple, the hotel's details are anything but: contemporary artwork, Egyptian cotton linens of an almost dizzying thread count, open-air showers, and a seaside location just steps from the surf. Choose from a long list of outdoor adventures (kayaking; dune buggy drives; horseback rides along the beach), then cool off in the hotel's infinity pool. Come late afternoon, follow the villagers to the towering Pôr do Sol, or Sunset Dune, for the most stunning light show around.
Rua da Igreja; 55-88/9909-9135; chilibeach.com; doubles from $$$, including breakfast.

The Grand Salon at the
Shangri-La Hotel, Paris.

europe

COT LONDON LYNDHURST SINTRA MONROYO BARCELONA PARIS ST.-TROPE
MATUELLE MILAN FIESOLE ROME SICILY VALLETTA FLIMS LAAX FALERA BER
IDELBERG GHENT VALLDAL FURILLEN ST. PETERSBURG BUDAPEST CRETE EP
DRUM UÇHISAR ASCOT LONDON LYNDHURST SINTRA MONROYO BARCELO
RIS ST.-TROPEZ RAMATUELLE MILAN FIESOLE ROME SICILY VALLETTA FLIMS I
LERA BERLIN HEIDELBERG GHENT VALLDAL FURILLEN ST. PETERSBURG BUD
ETE EPIRUS BODRUM UÇHISAR ASCOT LONDON LYNDHURST SINTRA MONI

The bridge leading to Coworth Park's Barn restaurant. Opposite, from top: A custom copper soaking tub; the Drawing Room, where afternoon tea is served.

COWORTH PARK

Ascot, England

THE DORCHESTER COLLECTION'S PREVIOUS PROPERTIES LEAN more toward the urbane than the pastoral, so the group's latest opening—a classic English country house—brings new sophistication to the genre. On 240 acres in Ascot, 45 minutes from central London, the 70-room Coworth Park is made up of an 18th-century mansion, former stables, and cottages. (Most distinctive of all: the gabled Dower House, a three-bedroom residence with its own swan-filled stream.) Organic treatments by Dr. Alkaitis and a "living roof" planted with lavender and chamomile lend an eco-emphasis to the spa. Meals are some of the best you'll find outside London, thanks to three restaurants run by award-winning U.K. chef John Campbell, known for his experimental approach to cooking. A walk across the premises feels like wandering through a Jane Austen novel: all sunken gardens, dewy fields, and groves of lime trees fluttering in the breeze. The crack of mallets on the polo field is the only thing disturbing the silence. *Blacknest Rd.; 800/650-1842 or 44-1344/876-600; coworthpark.com; doubles from $$, including breakfast.*

spotlight london

THE CAPITAL OF COOL BRITANNIA shows no sign of slowing down, with one highly anticipated hotel opening after another. Perhaps no one does buzz better than the Soho House Group, whose 39-room Dean Street Townhouse puts a mod spin on quaint aristocracy. Reimagined Georgian interiors—hand-painted wallpaper, pedestal tubs, and gleaming silver tea sets—mark each space, and rooms range in designation from Broom Cupboard to Bigger. On the Strand, the Savoy's $350 million redo has been billed as the most ambitious hotel restoration in British history, drawing upon historical Edwardian and Art Deco references to update the iconic 1889 structure. Not to be missed:

The Much Bigger Room at Dean Street Townhouse.

Afternoon tea in the Savoy's Upper Thames Foyer.

DEAN STREET TOWNHOUSE

69-71 Dean St.; 44-20/7434-1775; deanstreettownhouse. com; doubles from $.

the black and gold Beaufort Bar, which stands on the site of the hotel's original cabaret stage and offers the city's most extensive by-the-glass champagne menu. In the hub of the West End, the Langham recently underwent a $125 million refurbishment, including a new lobby and a spa in a former bank vault. Afternoon tea is still served daily in the Palm Court (where the tradition was reportedly born), with a selection of sandwiches, scones, pastries, and mini-cakes. With a guest book that runs the gamut from Mark Twain and Oscar Wilde to Peter Sellers, this grande dame seems poised to continue its storied legacy.

The sitting area in the Langham's Portland Suite.

THE SAVOY

Strand; 800/441-1414 or 44-20/7836-4343; fairmont.com/ savoy; doubles from $$$$.

THE LANGHAM

1C Portland Place; 800/588-9141 or 44-20/7636-1000; langhamhotels.com; doubles from $$$$.

LIME WOOD

Lyndhurst, England

SPENDING A WEEKEND IN WELLIES NEVER FELT MORE STYLISH THAN at this handsome Hampshire spread, which strikes an admirable balance between heritage and design. The red-brick Regency main structure, built on the site of a 13th-century hunting lodge, features cream-and-*eau-de-nil*-hued interiors by David Collins, who created the Blue Bar at the Berkeley in London. Additional buildings, including the three-story Herb House spa, were designed by architect Charles Morris, known for his work on Prince Charles's Highgrove residence. Add former Soho House Group director Robin Hutson as chairman and London chef Luke Holder, who trained at the Michelin three-starred Enoteca Pinchiorri in Italy, and it's clear that rural England is alive with fresh energy. *Beaulieu Rd.; 800/735-2478 or 44-23/8028-7177; limewood hotel.co.uk; doubles from $$.*

Strolling the garden at Lime Wood.

HOTEL TIVOLI PALÁCIO DE SETEAIS

Sintra, Portugal

LESS THAN AN HOUR NORTH OF LISBON, Sintra was once the summer playground of Portugal's kings. In the 1950's, the Hotel Tivoli Palácio de Seteais—the 18th-century residence of the Dutch consul—opened as a gilded Neoclassical resort with frescoed walls and copious antiques, attracting a who's who of cinematic royalty over the years (Catherine Deneuve; John Malkovich). Of late, it has undergone a meticulous restoration, with updated in-room technology that's all the more impressive when juxtaposed against the panoramas of Moorish palaces and castles. Settle down to a glass of wine at the bar's outdoor terrace, then allow the hotel's Experience Managers to arrange the next day's activities: a sail down the coast, a tour of the sights from a 1930's replica sidecar, or a private dinner at the nearby Capuchos Convent.
8 Avda. Barbosa du Bocage; 351-21/923-3200; tivolihotels.com; doubles from $$, including breakfast.

The front garden at Hotel
Tivoli Palácio de Seteais.

The pool at Consolación.
Opposite: Detached
"Kube" guest cabins.

CONSOLACIÓN

Monroyo, Spain

IN THE SOUTHERN REACHES OF ARAGÓN, a two-hour train ride from Barcelona and Valencia, Consolación capitalizes on its setting brilliantly. Spanish design firm Camprubí i Santacana Arquitectes transformed a 16th-century hillside hermitage into a series of pared-down common areas and two guest rooms—one an homage to Nordic Modernism, complete with Alvar Aalto light fixtures; the other inspired by 19th-century Romanticism, featuring velvet wingback chairs and an enormous, gilt-framed oil painting. Even more noteworthy are the 10 freestanding Kube suites, each with a glass wall and a balcony looking out across a valley of pine and olive trees. True to its ecclesiastical past, minimalist interior details (sunken slate tubs; fireplaces suspended from the ceiling) remain conducive to contemplation. Grab a picnic lunch from the hotel kitchen, where a fridge is kept stocked for guests, and wend your way along footpaths fragrant with rosemary and thyme. You'll end up at a stunner of a swimming pool carved out of the cliff.
Km 96, Crta. Nacional 232; 34/97-885-6755; consolacion.com.es; doubles from $, including breakfast.

MANDARIN ORIENTAL BARCELONA

Barcelona

THE FIRST SOUTHERN EUROPEAN OUTPOST FOR THE MANDARIN ORIENTAL GROUP is a distinctly multicultural collaboration. In Barcelona's elegant Eixample district, of-the-moment Spanish designer Patricia Urquiola oversaw the conversion of a mid-century bank building where an ascending walkway from the entrance to the lobby cuts through the light-filled atrium. The 98 rooms are a harmonious marriage of clean-lined modernity and Asian accents: modular white leather furniture and neutral French carpeting offset black lacquer tables; brushed-steel lighting fixtures counter gauzy screens and delicate metal latticework. The spa offers holistic treatments that range from Chinese healing therapies to native citrus, wild mint, and olive oil body scrubs. At the helm of the hotel restaurant is Raül Balam, son of Catalan chef Carme Ruscalleda—one of the few women in the world to amass five Michelin stars for her two restaurants. *38-40 Passeig de Gràcia; 800/526-6566 or 34/93-151-8888; mandarinoriental.com; doubles from $$.*

Mandarin Oriental Barcelona's Blanc restaurant. Opposite: A view of the city from the penthouse terrace.

A staff member at Le Royal Monceau's front desk. Left: Le Grand Salon, the hotel's lobby.

LE ROYAL MONCEAU, RAFFLES PARIS

Paris

PHILIPPE STARCK'S WHIMSICAL, THEATRICAL DESIGN STYLINGS meet an unapologetically luxe sensibility at the refurbished Le Royal Monceau. The 149 rooms re-create the romance of the mid 20th century with plush textures, eclectic lamps, and chic French furnishings that look sublimely livable; an acoustic guitar in each room and poetic inscriptions on desks lend artistic inspiration. Public spaces are designed to make an iconoclastic statement. A private screening room is modeled after an airplane's first-class section, and has one lipstick-red chair placed deliberately among the 98 dove-gray seats. The bold shell motif throughout the restaurant Il Carpaccio, within the hotel's garden, calls to mind a Sicilian grotto. Lower-profile, but no less welcome, are the streamlined sofas and side tables, which invite visitors to linger over drinks beneath Le Grand Salon's ornate chandeliers.

37 Ave. Hoche, Eighth Arr.; 800/768-9009 or 33-1/42-99-88-00; raffles.com; doubles from $$$$.

A Cassina couch and Noguchi table in the Intercontinental Paris Avenue Marceau's Terrace Suite. Left: Venetian frescoes on a Deluxe room ceiling.

INTERCONTINENTAL PARIS AVENUE MARCEAU

Paris

FOR ALL ITS REFINEMENT, THE LATEST FIVE-STAR HOTEL TO ARRIVE IN PARIS is not at all uptight. First, there's its size—at just 55 rooms, the InterContinental Paris Avenue Marceau feels much more intimate than many of the brand's sister properties. Then there's its style. Set in the former residence of a Parisian count, with a Cubist painting by Raymond Moretti offsetting the Baccarat table and Murano chandeliers in the lobby, the hotel contrasts impeccably chosen antiques with pieces by Modernist masters, including Isamu Noguchi and Le Corbusier. The restaurant, run by a former sous-chef at the George V, forgoes overly elaborate concoctions for a polished twist on comfort food: try the club sandwich with black truffles or the duck pie served with root vegetables, both as deceptively simple as they are delicious.
64 Ave. Marceau, Eighth Arr.; 800/327-0200 or 33-1/44-43-36-42; intercontinental.com; doubles from $$$.

SHANGRI-LA HOTEL, PARIS

Paris

IT'S JUST WHAT YOU'D EXPECT FROM A RESIDENCE THAT ONCE belonged to a Bonaparte prince. For the newest addition to its roster, the Hong Kong–based Shangri-La hotel group enlisted interior designer Pierre-Yves Rochon, who created the look of Paris's George V and London's recently restored Savoy, to enhance the already impressive wow factor of the 1896 building. The 81 rooms and suites feature marble bathrooms with heated floors and Empire-style furniture and wallpaper; many of the sweeping skyline vistas include cinematic Eiffel Tower views. Sign up for an in-suite Asian-inspired treatment, or go for a swim in the 50-foot-long pool, which is bathed in natural light and overlooks a garden that was formerly the entrance to the prince's stables. Afterward, feast on indulgent French and Cantonese dishes—plus wine from the hotel's expansive cellar—the way a true Parisian would: without an ounce of guilt.

10 Ave. d'Iéna; 866/565-5050 or 33-1/53-67-19-98; shangri-la.com; doubles from $$$$.

The main entrance to the Shangri-La
Hotel, Paris. Opposite: Viewing the Eiffel
Tower from the Chaillot Suite's terrace.

spotlight
the french riviera

FROM THE MOMENT BIKINI-CLAD BRIGITTE BARDOT MADE HER big-screen debut, St.-Tropez has been synonymous with the international jet set. Here, yachting is more than a pastime; it's a way of life—as evidenced by the billionaires and their retinues who disembark each evening to mingle in the lounges of some of the world's most extraordinary resorts. Yet even in this most glamorous of enclaves, four relative newcomers are making a splash on the hotel scene. This year, famous friends like Chloë Sevigny and Christian Louboutin will help French graffiti artist Monsieur André decorate the slick, Technicolor rooms at Hôtel Ermitage, whose casual bistro draws celebrity crowds. Nearby, you'll find a Dom Pérignon champagne bar inside the Hôtel Sezz Saint-Tropez, a cluster of modern villas and poolside suites designed by Philippe Starck protégé Christophe Pillet. At Zen-inspired Muse Luxury Hôtel, in neighboring Ramatuelle, the ivory-hued guest quarters open onto a terraced garden overlooking the Mediterranean. (To reach the beach, hop on one of the hotel's bikes or take the free shuttle: a Bentley.) Privacy seekers flock to La Réserve Ramatuelle, a minimalist oasis with white-and-beige rooms and an 11,000-square-foot spa hidden in the pine-covered hills outside town. A Crème de La Mer facial or an energizing treatment will prepare you for the evening at hand. This is, after all, the French Riviera, and the action starts after dark.

The red-lacquered corridor near Hôtel Ermitage's room No. 19.

La Réserve Ramatuelle's bird's-eye view of the Mediterranean.

A sculpture by Celia Gouveiac at Hôtel Sezz Saint-Tropez.

Cabanas and sun beds in Muse Luxury Hôtel's pool area.

HÔTEL ERMITAGE

Ave. Paul Signac, St.-Tropez; 33-4/94-97-52-33; ermitagehotel.fr; doubles from $$.

HÔTEL SEZZ
SAINT-TROPEZ

Rte. des Salins, St.-Tropez; 800/337-4685 or 33-4/94-55-31-55; hotelsezz-sainttropez.com; doubles from $$$.

MUSE LUXURY HÔTEL

Rte. des Marres, Ramatuelle; 33-4/94-43-04-40; muse-hotels.com; doubles from $$$$$.

LA RÉSERVE
RAMATUELLE HÔTEL,
SPA & VILLAS

Chemin de la Quessine, Ramatuelle; 33-4/94-44-94-44; lareserve-ramatuelle.com; doubles from $$$$$.

The Sleeping in a Ballgown Room.
Above: An origami lamp punctuates
Maison Moschino's six-story staircase.

MAISON MOSCHINO

Milan

IT'S ONLY FITTING THAT THE MOST TALKED-ABOUT NEW PROPERTY in Italy's style capital is from a homegrown fashion house. Set within a Neoclassical former train station near the busy Corso Como neighborhood and designed by two of the label's top creative talents, Maison Moschino is true to the brand's playful approach. The 65-room hotel is rife with surrealistic flourishes, including 16 fairy tale–themed suites meant to inspire dreams (an oversize Edison bulb above a teacup table in Alice's Room; tree-trunk beds against trompe l'oeil woods in the aptly named Forest Suite). Much of the décor is even available for sale in the boutique, including the petal-covered bedspreads in the Life is a Bed of Roses Room. The fun continues at Clandestino Milano restaurant, where extra-virgin olive oil, balsamic vinegar, tomatoes, and *burrata* cheese are rendered into "susci" rolls, chef Moreno Cedroni's take on classic maki sushi. *12 Viale Monte Grappa; 39-02/2900-9858; maisonmoschino. com; doubles from $$$.*

Faux trees anchor the bed in the Forest Suite.

The exterior of Il Salviatino, surrounded by cypress and pine trees.

IL SALVIATINO

Fiesole, Italy

THE NOBLE SALVIATI FAMILY TOOK OWNERSHIP of a sumptuous country villa on the northeastern outskirts of Florence in the 16th century. Last year, after painstaking renovations that revealed long-lost frescoes on the ceilings and hidden pathways twisting through 12 acres of gardens, hotelier Marcello Pigozzo Sr. reopened the aristocratic abode as a 45-room property that rivals Villa San Michele. Barrel-vaulted ceilings, oak parquet floors, and mosaic-tiled soaking tubs blend seamlessly into the space, complemented by hand-loomed Tuscan bed linens and museum-worthy oil paintings. Some of the largest suites are in jewel box–like greenhouses with direct access to the gardens. In the midst of such Renaissance grandeur, the hotel maintains a residential feel. There is no reception desk, and guests are welcome to dine wherever they choose—whether in the wood-paneled library or on one of the white leather chesterfields on the terrace, perfectly positioned to maximize expansive views of the Duomo.

21 Via del Salviatino; 39-055/904-1111; salviatino.com; doubles from $$$, including breakfast.

The living room at Casa Manni Roma. Left: Rome's Via di Pietra.

CASA MANNI ROMA

Rome

WHEN IN ROME, YOU CAN NOW LIVE LIKE A ROMAN—a well-connected one at that. The one-bedroom penthouse of olive-oil maker and bon vivant Armando Manni provides an exclusive look at the Eternal City visitors rarely get to see. Located within walking distance of the Pantheon and Trevi Fountain, the Adam D. Tihany–designed dwelling is filled with patterned glass and Macassar ebony wood—a marvel in its own right. But the real draw is insider access to Manni's personal black book: Schedule a private ravioli-making class with Oretta Zanini de Vita, Italy's mistress of handmade pasta, or a decadent couples massage at Acanto, a spa favored by affluent locals. After a stroll through iconic sites accompanied by an art historian, retreat to the apartment's terrace, overlooking the Baroque rooftops of the Piazza Colonna.
70 Via di Pietra; 39-06/9727-4787; casamanni.com; daily rentals from $$$$$, including breakfast and spirits, two-night minimum.

VERDURA GOLF & SPA RESORT

Sciacca, Italy

Verdura Golf & Spa Resort's infinity pool and bar.

STILL RELATIVELY UNDISCOVERED, THE SOUTHWESTERN COAST OF SICILY—just 1½ hours outside Palermo—is a destination on the rise, thanks to a host of new hotels, including the Verdura, the first resort from the Rocco Forte Collection. The compound of low-slung, rectilinear sandstone buildings is set on 570 acres amid lemon and orange groves; each room has a private terrace and a sea view so spectacular that even expert golfers might not notice the three courses designed by Kyle Phillips. Polished concrete floors and white-canopied beds are interrupted by bursts of orange and yellow, as well as local majolica and ironwork. Also on the grounds is a square with a 15th-century watchtower, a pizzeria and gelateria, and Lady Aliai Forte's well-curated boutique (look for examples of the region's traditional lace). At the 43,000-square-foot spa, a massage of lemongrass- and zagara-infused olive oil hits all the right notes. *Km 131, S.S. 115; 888/667-9477 or 39-0925/998-001; verduraresort.com; doubles from $$$$, including breakfast.*

A crystal chandelier in one of Maison La Vallette's bathrooms. Left: Bedrooms reinterpret traditional Maltese residences.

MAISON LA VALLETTE

Valletta, Malta

IS MALTA THE NEW CAPRI? THAT MIGHT SOON BE THE CASE now that a crop of cafés, wine bars, and hotels has opened in the formerly sleepy island nation. The best place to stay is Maison La Vallette, a bohemian town house set within the capital city's UNESCO-protected medieval walls. One of three unique accommodations owned by design duo Brian Grech and Stephen Azzopardi, Maison is part of a mission to restore small living spaces within the city. Guests are given free rein over a house that blends Baroque Maltese architecture with quirky touches: gaudy gilded chandeliers hanging from wood-beamed ceilings; tongue-in-cheek renderings of Renaissance portraits adorning exposed limestone walls. LCD TV's, bespoke decoupage furniture, and Kartell lamps conjure up a modern mix, while king-size Pierre Cardin beds afford optimum comfort. And with a spacious kitchen at your disposal, shopping for provisions is a pleasure—the narrow, atmospheric streets beckon with local greengrocers and bakeries.
2 St. Patrick St.; 356/7948-8047; maisonlavallette.com; doubles from $.

A guest room at Rocksresort's Signinahotel. Right: The resort's quartzite façade.

ROCKSRESORT

Flims Laax Falera, Switzerland

SWISS HOTELIER RETO GURTNER MAY BEAR MORE THAN A PASSING RESEMBLANCE to a mad yodeler. But at Rocksresort, located below Flims Laax Falera's sprawling ski slopes, the snowboard aficionado has forsaken traditional Tyrolean gingerbread for a rough-hewn façade that puts a conceptual spin on the classic landscape. Eight cube-shaped buildings, arranged to mimic the aftermath of a landslide, house 122 apartment-style units with minimalist interiors: gnarled oak walls, lime putty floors, and soaring windows. A Ski Direct client card allows guests to collect points on purchases (lift tickets; ski rentals) that can later be redeemed for air miles and other rewards. At the complex's five restaurants, offerings range from pan-Asian cuisine to traditional Swiss raclette grilled over an open fire. Après-ski, choose between a mellow evening of frothy beer served in steins or a late-night dance party backed by international DJ's.
Talstation; 41-81/927-9999; rocksresort.com; doubles from $, four- or seven-night minimum during winter.

A patron at Michelberger Hotel's coffee shop, which doubles as a bar.

The shop's bookshelves, stocked with German design magazines. Below: Irreverent door signs.

MICHELBERGER HOTEL

Berlin

NO ONE CAN DENY THE MICHELBERGER'S INDIE CRED. Built in a refashioned factory in Berlin's Friedrichshain neighborhood, the hotel feels more like a large-scale art-school project, with custom-made furniture and clever loftlike setups that make the most of the 119 rooms' every square inch. Unlike a lot of self-conscious lodgings around the world, this one exudes effortless style. Inside, the Wi-Fi is free, the coffee is gourmet, and hallway TV's play a permanent loop of *The Big Lebowski*. Outside, a small courtyard acts as both beer garden and concert venue. Though the place is billed as a sort of "intergalactic" hub—glowing crystal orbs are suspended from the dining-room ceiling; hanging installations in the bar evoke lunar modules—the result is less outer space and more like your coolest friend's crash pad. *39/40 Warschauerstrasse; 49-30/2977-8590; michelberger hotel.com; doubles from $.*

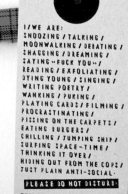

HEIDELBERG SUITES

Heidelberg, Germany

WITH ITS CASTLE RUINS AND MEDIEVAL SQUARES, Heidelberg has lured poets and philosophers for ages. Now Heidelberg Suites, a 19th-century villa converted by Florentine architect Michele Bönan, has made this storybook town a magnet for design-obsessed travelers as well. The front-and-center views of Old Town are stunning, but you'll also find yourself admiring the interiors, a study in Neoclassical-inspired décor (etched mirrors; Roman busts) complemented by warm gray walls and custom Italian furniture. The 25 guest rooms and lounge area are filled with vintage books and art magazines. Docked only a few steps away, a refurbished 1930's yacht serves as the hotel's restaurant, an ideal place to sip aperitifs as you drift down the River Neckar.
12 Neuenheimer Landstrasse; 49-6221/655-650; heidelbergsuites.com; doubles from $$, including breakfast.

Understated furnishings at
Heidelberg Suites. Opposite:
The fireplace in the lounge and
breakfast room.

SCONES
€ 2,50

Simon Turner, co-owner
of Simon Says, at the
hotel's downstairs café.

SIMON SAYS

Ghent, Belgium

ITS FLEMISH SISTERS ANTWERP AND BRUGES MAY BE BETTER KNOWN,
but the university town of Ghent has the best of both
worlds: restaurants and boutiques to rival the former,
and centuries-old cobblestoned streets similar to those
found in the latter. The hotel culture here was once
dominated by generic chains, but the past few years have
seen an explosion of chic inns—including Simon Says,
a bed-and-breakfast above a coffeehouse in a 1904 Art
Nouveau building. British transplants Simon Turner and
Christopher Joseph kitted out two rooms with sandstone
bathrooms and light fixtures from the 1920's, and pride
themselves on an inviting welcome; they'll arrange
for pickups at the train station, recommend their favorite
galleries, shops, and bars, and book you a spa treatment
nearby. But the real treat comes each morning, when
you're greeted by name at the café and served fresh
Belgian coffee and all the pastries you can eat.
*8 Sluizeken; 32-9/233-0343; simon-says.be; doubles from $,
including breakfast.*

The glass-walled Per Eide studio
at Juvet Landscape Hotel.

JUVET
LANDSCAPE
HOTEL

Valldal, Norway

GETTING UP CLOSE AND PERSONAL WITH THE GREAT OUTDOORS
takes on new meaning at this series of glass-and-wood
structures on a mountain in northwestern Norway, about
an eight-hour drive from Oslo. Perched on steel pylons
above the Gudbrandsjuvet ravine and Valldøla River, the
seven stand-alone guest rooms have sleek spruce interiors,
Japanese-Norwegian-designed Stokke Tok recliners, and
floor-to-ceiling windows overlooking the rugged panorama.
Take part in a number of adventures: climbing and
rappelling courses in neighboring Reinheimen National
Park; excursions to local farms; and guided off-piste ski
treks even in the height of summer. A converted cowshed
serves as the dining room, a sheep barn will soon be a
lounge, and a contemporary-looking spa provides a modern
way to take the waters. With little else to distract you, your
immersion in nature is complete.
Gudbrandsjuvet; 47/9503-2010; juvet.com; doubles from $$,
including breakfast.

**Philippe Starck for Duravit
amenities in a studio bathroom.
Above: A guest room hallway.**

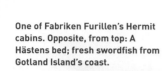

One of Fabriken Furillen's Hermit cabins. Opposite, from top: A Hästens bed; fresh swordfish from Gotland Island's coast.

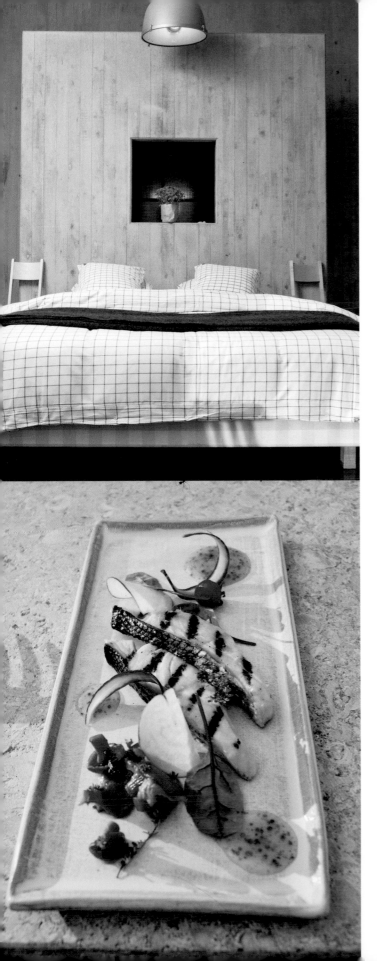

FABRIKEN FURILLEN

Furillen, Sweden

THE PLEASURES ARE SIMPLE ON THE TINY ISLET OF FURILLEN, off Sweden's Gotland Island: fresh seafood, deserted beaches, and Fabriken Furillen, a former limestone quarry transformed into the country's farthest-flung design hotel. Bang & Olufsen stereos, flat-screen TV's, open fireplaces, and metal clothes lockers lend an industrial edge to the main house's 16 rooms, while locally sourced sheepskin rugs, Hästens-made beds, and handcrafted Scandinavian furniture warm up the six seemingly spare Hermit Cabins, located a 20-minute walk from the main building. There's also a new chrome Airstream trailer for rent, with an eat-in kitchen and a double bed. Embark on an autumnal truffle hunt or simply spend the afternoon exploring the grounds on the hotel's Swedish-made Skeppshult bicycles. *Lärbro; 46-498/223-040; furillen.nu; doubles from $$, including breakfast; open April to mid-December.*

The garden seating area at Alexander House Boutique Hotel. Left: The first-floor lounge.

ALEXANDER HOUSE BOUTIQUE HOTEL

St. Petersburg, Russia

INTIMATE AND UNDERSTATED AREN'T WORDS TYPICALLY ASSOCIATED WITH RUSSIAN HOTELS—which makes Alexander House a rare find indeed. Owner Alexander Zhukov, a former war correspondent for the Associated Press, converted a 19th-century mansion two miles from Palace Square into a charming 19-room boutique inn. Zhukov—half proprietor, half patriarch—and his wife preside over affairs with a distinctly personal touch: books from his own multilingual collection adorn the library's shelves, journalist pals are regular fixtures, and the 24-hour kitchen cooks up traditional Russian and European dishes, from Ukrainian borscht to baked dorado with Provence herbs. Each of the rooms is named for a global city; ask for one on the second floor with views of the canal. A flower-filled garden in the inner courtyard provides the perfect summertime sanctuary, while during the snowy winters, guests find themselves happily ensconced by the lounge's roaring fire.
27 Kryukov Canal Embankment; 7-812/334-3540; a-house.ru; doubles from $$, including breakfast.

A guest room at Soho Boutique Hotel.

SOHO BOUTIQUE HOTEL

Budapest

THE CAPITAL OF HUNGARY IS SLOWLY SWAPPING ITS IRON CURTAIN GRIT for European panache. Case in point: the Soho Boutique Hotel, a retro-mod refuge in the heart of the city's cultural hub, mere minutes from the shops of Váci Street. Neon lights aside, the property's red-brick exterior could pass for the façade of a humdrum office building. But inside, the 74 guest rooms and suites are laid-back and hip, thanks to orange bucket chairs, Pop art murals, and earth-toned throw rugs on Swedish oak floors. On the other end of the style spectrum, two Baroque-style Vampire suites inspired by a musical remake of a Roman Polanski film—one has purple wallpaper and a golden armchair; the other, black candelabras dripping with crystals—are sure to appeal to *Twilight* fans and readers of Anne Rice. Campy, yes, but also strangely apropos in a city steeped in old-world mystery.

64 Dohány Utca; 36-1/872-8292; sohoboutiquehotel.com; doubles from $, including breakfast.

AMMOS HOTEL

Crete, Greece

IT'S ALL IN THE FAMILY AT THE AMMOS, A DOWN-TO-EARTH HAVEN amid a string of jumbo-size beach resorts, near Venetian Harbor in western Crete. Owner Nikos Tsepetis, whose father bought the site in the 1970's as a summer retreat for his brood, melded Scandinavian influences with a classic Greek aesthetic (stone walkways; whitewashed exteriors). Each of the 33 suites comes with its own kitchenette and is done up in a stark gray-and-white palette with playful adornments—a mustard-yellow wall here, a hit of Marimekko fabric there. Tsepetis's excellent local contacts make him an invaluable resource for planning day trips to ancient Knossos, the Byzantine monastery of Ayia Triada, or the ruins at Aptera. But with a quiet (and kid-friendly) stretch of shallow beach right outside your door and a seaside taverna serving irresistible snacks such as fried zucchini balls, you may just decide to stay put for your entire visit.
Glaros Beach, Chania; 30-2821/033-003; ammoshotel.com; doubles from $.

The beachfront restaurant. Opposite:
Mosaic tiles in the reception area of
the Ammos Hotel.

140

A view of Vikos Gorge from a suite at Aristi Mountain Resort.

9

Espresso freddo at Salvia restaurant. Below: Guest room walls made with quarry-cut rock.

ARISTI MOUNTAIN RESORT

Epirus, Greece

IN A PICTURESQUE PROVINCE OF NORTHWESTERN GREECE, 42 villages teeter over the majestic Vikos Gorge, said to be the world's deepest. Local laws protect the original architecture of the stone buildings, including the Aristi, an 18-room hotel that occupies the highest point in town. Most rooms are spare yet cozy, with hardwood floors and ceilings; book a suite to admire the rocky landscape from a separate, firelit living area. By day, scale the footpaths of the Gamila mountain range or raft the Voidomatis River that slices through the terrain. You'll work up an appetite for the rustic regional dishes for which the hotel's restaurant, Salvia, is known: *pites* (savory pies wrapped in thick, house-made phyllo dough), wild boar, smoked trout, and mountain greens sourced from the surrounding countryside.
44016 Aristi; 30-265/304-1330; aristi.eu; doubles from $.

MAÇAKIZI

Bodrum, Turkey

ON A PENINSULA WITH ITS SHARE OF OVER-THE-TOP RESORTS, Maçakizi is a sexy standout. More like the seaside estate of some globetrotting Turkish family, the property unfolds along a hillside studded with olive trees, tangerine groves, and bursts of bougainvillea. The 81 whitewashed guest rooms are minimally furnished and enhanced by the bold, abstract canvases of native painter Suat Akdemir; the beach club, a series of wooden decks shaded by sailcloth canopies and sheltered within a placid cove, resembles a magazine fashion shoot come to life. Every so often the muezzin's call to prayer drifts across the water from the town mosque, a trebly counterpoint to the languid jazz playing at the bar.

Kesire Mevkii, Türkbükü; 90-252/377-6272; macakizi.com; doubles from $$, including breakfast.

A guest emerging from Türkbükü Bay at Maçakizi. Opposite: Sunbathers on the resort's beach patio.

ARGOS IN CAPPADOCIA

Uçhisar, Turkey

IN THE MOUNTAINOUS REGION OF CAPPADOCIA, NEARLY ALL OF
the buildings were originally carved out of centuries-old
volcanic rock. Here, four 2,000-year-old mansions in the
hillside village of Uçhisar have been converted into a
luxury cave hotel, and despite such 21st-century amenities
as central heating and Wi-Fi, the arched ceilings and
hand-carved wall niches remain faithful to the past. Indoor
private plunge pools make the Splendid suites worth the
splurge; after a soak in the 91-degree water, you'll want
to do little more than settle in with a good book. On some
evenings, classical, jazz, and Sufi music recitals are
performed next door in the acoustically stellar Bezirhane
concert hall. Beneath it lies an ancient network of tunnels
and cellars, once part of a vast series of subterranean
dwellings now accessible via guided tour.
*23 Kayabasi Sokak; 90-384/219-3130; argosincappadocia.com;
doubles from $, including breakfast.*

Argos in Cappadocia's stone
terraces and gardens.

Qasr Al Sarab Desert Resort, in Abu Dhabi, United Arab Emirates.

africa & the middle east

MARRAKESH PHINDA PRIVATE GAME RESERVE CAPE TOWN ZANZIBAR ISLA
JERUSALEM BEIRUT MA'IN ABU DHABI DUBAI MAHE ILE DES DEUX COCOS M
PHINDA PRIVATE GAME RESERVE CAPE TOWN ZANZIBAR ISLAND JERUSALE
BEIRUT MA'IN ABU DHABI DUBAI MAHE ILE DES DEUX COCOS MARRAKESH
PRIVATE GAME RESERVE CAPE TOWN ZANZIBAR ISLAND JERUSALEM BEIRUT
DHABI DUBAI MAHE ILE DES DEUX COCOS MARRAKESH PHINDA PRIVATE G
RESERVE CAPE TOWN ZANZIBAR ISLAND JERUSALEM BEIRUT MA'IN ABU DH

148

The Moroccan lounge in the lobby of the Royal Mansour Marrakech.

Room No. 3 at Riad El Fenn.

spotlight
marrakesh

ONCE IT WAS AN EXOTIC NORTH AFRICAN BACKWATER WHOSE
visitors were mostly hippies in search of cheap crash
pads and good hash. Now this city of medieval
souks and winding streets is undergoing a dramatic
transformation, its ramshackle *riads* giving way to lavish
boutique hotels. In the medina, Morocco's royal family
spared no expense on Royal Mansour Marrakech, a
cluster of 53 town houses with silk-paneled walls, tiled
fireplaces, and roof terraces featuring bedouin tents and
wading pools. The more intimately scaled Riad Siwan
is a former palace made up of seven large guest rooms
decorated with locally made furniture and one-of-a-
kind handblown glass lamps. British hotelier Jonathan
Wix's Riad Farnatchi was so popular that he expanded
the property into an adjacent mansion; set around a
maze of courtyards, the nine suites combine Modernist
furniture with sunken bathtubs and Berber carpets.
Meanwhile, Vanessa Branson (sister of Sir Richard) and
Howell James have tripled the size of Riad El Fenn, one
of the flashiest addresses in town. Favored by the media
and art-world elite, the hotel has 21 rooms spread across
three palaces, with modern works by British painter
Bridget Riley scattered throughout. With three pools, a
rooftop putting green, and a small screening room, Riad
El Fenn is just one symbol of Marrakesh's new status as
a desert crossroads at the cutting edge.

A marble fountain in the courtyard at Riad Siwan.

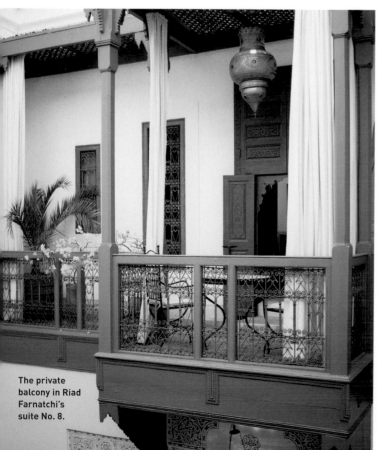

The private balcony in Riad Farnatchi's suite No. 8.

ROYAL MANSOUR MARRAKECH

Rue Abou Abbas el Sebti, Medina; 800/223-6800 or 212-529/808-080; royalmansour.com; riads from $$$$$.

RIAD SIWAN

28 Zanka Adika, Riad Zitoun Jdid, Medina; 212-661/158-173; riadsiwan.com; doubles from $$, including breakfast.

RIAD FARNATCHI

2 Derb el Farnatchi, Medina; 212-524/384-910; riadfarnatchi. com; doubles from $$.

RIAD EL FENN

2 Derb Moulay Abdellah Ben Hezzian, Medina; 212-524/441-210; riadelfenn.com; doubles from $$, including breakfast.

The lounge at Homestead, made with such traditional materials as thatch, gumpole, and stone tile.

The villa's open-air shower and bath area.
Below: Decorative floor lamps in the lounge.

HOMESTEAD AT &BEYOND PHINDA PRIVATE GAME RESERVE

South Africa

THERE'S NO NEED TO RISE FOR A PRESCHEDULED EARLY-MORNING game drive when you're staying at Homestead, a private, fully staffed villa from luxury safari outfitter &Beyond. With a guide, a tracker, and a 4 x 4 at your disposal, you set the hours for field forays in search of cheetahs and black rhinos on this 56,000-acre reserve in South Africa's northeastern coastal woodlands. Or let the wildlife come to you: the villa is set on the edge of a pan that fills with water seasonally, so elephants will be drawn to your doorstep. The four expansive, glass-sided suites are decorated with pieces made by local Zulu tribesmen, including *imfebengi* bead chandeliers and *assegai* (spears) mounted on the walls. Such bush specialties as *boeboetie*, a spicy beef dish, and a plate of sticky doughnuts called *koeksuster* are worthy additions to the menu. And if a deep-sea dive strikes your fancy? A 10-minute ride in the resort's helicopter brings you straight from the savanna to the coast for a daylong excursion on the Sodwana Bay reefs. *Phinda Private Game Reserve; 888/882-4742 or 27-11/809-4300; andbeyond.com; villas from $$$$$ for four, all-inclusive.*

A Table Mountain suite at One&Only Cape Town. Right: An aerial view of the hotel, on the Victoria and Alfred Waterfront.

ONE&ONLY CAPE TOWN

Cape Town, South Africa

YOU KNOW WHAT THEY SAY ABOUT FIRST IMPRESSIONS. So do the designers at One&Only Cape Town, who capped off the lobby with a 40-foot-tall picture window that frames a captivating view of Table Mountain. But then, outsize extravagance is trumpeted everywhere here, from the 5,000-bottle wine loft in Reuben's restaurant to the two private islands—one for the Balinese spa, the other for 40 suites outfitted in African wood and contemporary artwork. The first luxury hotel built in the city in nearly a decade is also home to Africa's premier Nobu restaurant and to Neo, a boutique that showcases designers from Pierre Hardy to Balenciaga. Upstairs, the 91 cream-colored rooms (Cape Town's largest) come with dedicated 24-hour butlers and your choice of scented pillows. Almost every feature is designed to impress— even the freestanding tubs, which have commanding marina vistas.

Dock Rd., Victoria & Alfred Waterfront; 866/552-0001 or 27-21/431-5888; oneandonlyresorts.com; doubles from $$$$, including breakfast.

Taj Cape Town's marble lobby.

TAJ CAPE TOWN

Cape Town, South Africa

HOUSED IN THE FORMER SOUTH AFRICAN RESERVE BANK HEADQUARTERS, a 1929 building in the heart of the city, the 177-room Taj Cape Town checks all the right boxes. Heritage rooms are spacious, with high ceilings and original mullioned windows. Tower rooms feel more compact but are equally desirable, thanks to floor-to-ceiling windows and walk-out balconies that put Table Mountain front and center. Meanwhile, the whole of Cape Town is clamoring for a seat at Bombay Brasserie, an outpost of the London original; exotically upholstered armchairs and glowing parquet floors set the scene for chef Harpreet Kaur's refined Indian dishes, from *bhalla chaat* (lentil dumplings in yogurt) to a slow-simmered leg of lamb. The Taj's location—just steps from Parliament and five blocks from the convention center—makes the restaurant a popular spot for power lunches. Clearly this is the business hotel to book.

Wale St.; 866/969-1825 or 27-21/819-2000; tajhotels.com; doubles from $$$, including breakfast.

KILINDI

Zanzibar Island, Tanzania

THE INDIAN OCEAN ISLAND OF ZANZIBAR IS KNOWN FOR ITS FRAGRANT SPICES, Swahili culture, and isolated beaches. Now it can add Kilindi to that list. On a 52-acre sun-bleached crescent, 15 domed stucco villas line a bay where wooden dhows (traditional Arab sailboats) still ply the aquamarine waters. With just 30 guests at a time, Kilindi's biggest draw is its exclusivity, but luxury comes with a light footprint—trade winds cool the sprawling white-on-white structures in place of air-conditioning, rainwater collected on the roofs runs into the pools, and a solar-powered plant treats wastewater that feeds the organic gardens. The on-site restaurant makes ample use of fresh fruit and local fish, and throughout the resort, the interior embellishments are simple: handwoven baskets, bleached wood, and seashells that echo the soothing palette of sand and sky. *Kendwa; 800/806-9565 or 255-27/250-0630; elewana.com; doubles from $$$$$, all-inclusive.*

The infinity pool at Kilindi. Opposite: One of the resort's whitewashed villas.

The sheet-metal staircase that connects Mamilla Hotel's three levels. Opposite: Jerusalem, as seen from the rooftop brasserie.

MAMILLA HOTEL

Jerusalem

FEW PLACES JUXTAPOSE THE OLD AND THE NEW BETTER THAN Jerusalem. Amid the Holy City's ancient buildings lie modern architectural icons—from Santiago Calatrava's Jerusalem Chords Bridge to architect Moshe Safdie's angular, elegant Mamilla Hotel. Interior designer Piero Lissoni kitted out the 194 rooms with dark oak floors, walls of luminous, pale stone, and furnishings from Kartell, Cassina, and Knoll. An innovative liquid-crystal wall separates bedrooms and bathrooms, the touch of a button providing instant privacy or transparency. In the spa, Akasha, a music meditation room, juice bar, and Watsu pool set a 21st-century mood. Still, the past has its place in the present: the amphitheater-style synagogue doubles as the hotel's private screening room.

11 King Solomon St.; 972-2/548-2200; mamillahotel.com; doubles from $$, including breakfast.

Indigo, Le Gray's rooftop restaurant, with views of the Mohammad Al-Amin mosque. Left: The hotel's romantically lit façade.

LE GRAY

Beirut, Lebanon

ONCE MORE, WAR-TORN BEIRUT IS UNDERGOING A REVIVAL, its grand mansions rising from the rubble. Le Gray, the latest property from British hotelier Gordon Campbell Gray, is at once a symbol of its progress and a perfect vantage point from which to take it all in. The 87 understated rooms feature mosaic tile floors and pieces by Arab, Cuban, and French artists; views are of the Hadiqat As-Samah garden, Mohammad Al-Amin mosque, and St. George's cathedral, a telling panorama of the town's complex history. On the roof, a purple-glass infinity pool and adjacent lounge draw a boldfaced crowd of fashion and showbiz insiders (Kevin Spacey, Christian Louboutin, and Bette Midler have been recent guests). It's further proof of the resurgence of this Mediterranean hot spot, surely one of the most resilient cities in the world.

Martyrs' Square; 961-1/971-111; legray.com; doubles from $$.

Evason Ma'In's heated swimming pool,
overlooking a natural hot spring.

EVASON MA'IN HOT SPRINGS &
SIX SENSES SPA

Ma'In, Jordan

WHERE ELSE CAN TRAVELERS HIKE AN AGE-OLD BEDOUIN TRAIL, view a chariot race in an 1,800-year-old Roman amphitheater, and bathe in the saline-rich waters of the Dead Sea? History, adventure, and wellness are the key offerings at the 97-room Evason Ma'In, located 866 feet below sea level in a valley framed by rocky cliffs and built around a spring-fed waterfall that runs into a thermal pool. In an effort to showcase Jordan's holy sites and natural and cultural attractions, the hotel curates a series of once-in-a-lifetime experiences: from a visit to the mosaic-making town of Madaba to a traditional Berber tented barbecue dinner in the desert. At the spa, treatments utilize mineral-rich mud and local ingredients such as olive oil, dates, and honey—although nothing beats the feeling of floating in the Dead Sea, a 30-minute shuttle ride away and perhaps the ultimate holistic day-trip.
Madaba; 962-5/324-5500; sixsenses.com; doubles from $$, including breakfast.

Qasr Al Sarab's crenellated exterior.

QASR AL SARAB DESERT RESORT BY ANANTARA

Abu Dhabi, United Arab Emirates

ONE OF THE PLANET'S LARGEST UNINTERRUPTED STRETCHES OF sand, the Empty Quarter of the Liwa Desert provides an awe-inspiring setting for Anantara's Qasr Al Sarab Desert Resort. The fortress-like, 206-unit complex rambles for more than a mile across the dunes—an Arabian oasis on par with the impeccably appointed Asian and South Seas properties (Thai jungle lodges; Maldivian overwater villas) for which the hotel group is known. The resort is a favored weekend spot for the region's glitterati. Helipads accommodate visiting Emirati sheikhs; everyone else arrives by car, a 125-mile ride from downtown Abu Dhabi. Jewel-toned textiles, bedouin artifacts, and hammered-brass vessels sourced from local souks give guest rooms a trade-route ambience. After a day spent traversing the desert on foot or camelback, return for a rejuvenating session in the spa's heated marble hammam and a pot of mint tea served beside the fountain at Liwan Lounge. *1 Qasr Al Sarab Rd.; 971-2/886-2088; anantara.com; doubles from $$.*

ARMANI HOTEL DUBAI

Dubai, United Arab Emirates

IN THIS LAND OF UNBRIDLED AMBITION, one tower stands high above the rest. Elegant and aloof, the 2,717-foot Burj Khalifa is the tallest building in the world—and the site of Giorgio Armani's first venture as a hotelier, where every inch embodies the understated look that is his signature. Echoing the minaret-like skyscraper itself, the 160 rooms curve and bend; one wall is leather, another fabric or wood. The hotel is a natural showcase for the designer's namesake enterprises, which range from flowers to sweets and flatware. Armani also dreamed up the property's eight restaurants, as well as a spa that opens onto an outdoor swimming pool ringed by charcoal-gray beach umbrellas. Some 600 employees from around the globe were aggressively recruited and meticulously trained to serve guests; youthful and cosmopolitan, they are all, of course, dressed entirely in Armani.
Burj Khalifa; 971-4/888-3888; armanihotels.com; doubles from $$$.

Burj Khalifa at dusk. Opposite:
Mediterraneo restaurant at
Armani Hotel Dubai.

Tree house villas at Four Seasons Resort Seychelles. Opposite, from top: Zez restaurant's kids' menu; Zez Lounge.

FOUR SEASONS RESORT SEYCHELLES

Mahé, Seychelles

THIS TREE HOUSE–STYLE GETAWAY, WITH ONE OF THE COUNTRY'S best white-sand beaches, is a design statement in true Four Seasons style. Set on forested slopes, the hotel group's first Seychelles outpost consists of 67 ocean-view villas with floor-to-ceiling sliding doors, plunge pools, and glass-walled rain showers that look out over stands of frangipani and cinnamon trees. An infinity pool and beach club lie at the base of the hill; midway up, the open-air restaurant Zez serves Middle Eastern–inspired dishes. On a ridge at the peak—262 feet above the beach—is a spa complex of five pavilions and eight tranquil treatment rooms, plus a rooftop yoga area that looks onto Petite Anse Bay. Despite the vertiginous layout, there's no need to worry about overexertion: chauffeurs in electric buggies whisk guests wherever they want to go.
Petite Anse, Baie Lazare; 800/332-3442 or 248/393-000; fourseasons.com; doubles from $$$$, including breakfast.

ILE DES DEUX COCOS

Ile des Deux Cocos, Mauritius

PERHAPS THE WORLD'S MOST SECLUDED RESORT, ILE DES DEUX
Cocos is hidden on a private 12-acre island off Mauritius's
southeastern coast. The Moorish-style villa was built nearly
a century ago as the weekend retreat of British governor
Sir Hesketh Bell, but these days the bright two-bedroom
manse makes the perfect spot for playing castaway in style.
A tiled interior courtyard gives onto a colonial-inspired
dining room, where the bay-window vistas are just as
impressive as the service; the full-time butler can also
arrange for lobster lunches on the sea-facing terrace or
candlelit dinners of grilled marlin by the bougainvillea-
fringed pool. Dining isn't your only option, though. Wend
through coconut groves to a string of deserted white-sand
beaches or take a quick speedboat ride to the protected
Blue Bay Maritime Reserve and Purple Cave, two of the
country's best dive sites. After a day spent exploring,
catch the sunset from a hammock back at the house while
sampling artisanal fruit-infused rums.
011-230/696-8866; naiade.com; doubles from $$$$$.

An aerial view of Ile des Deux Cocos, in the Indian Ocean.

A staff member greeting guests at the
Alila Villas Uluwatu in Bali, Indonesia.

asia

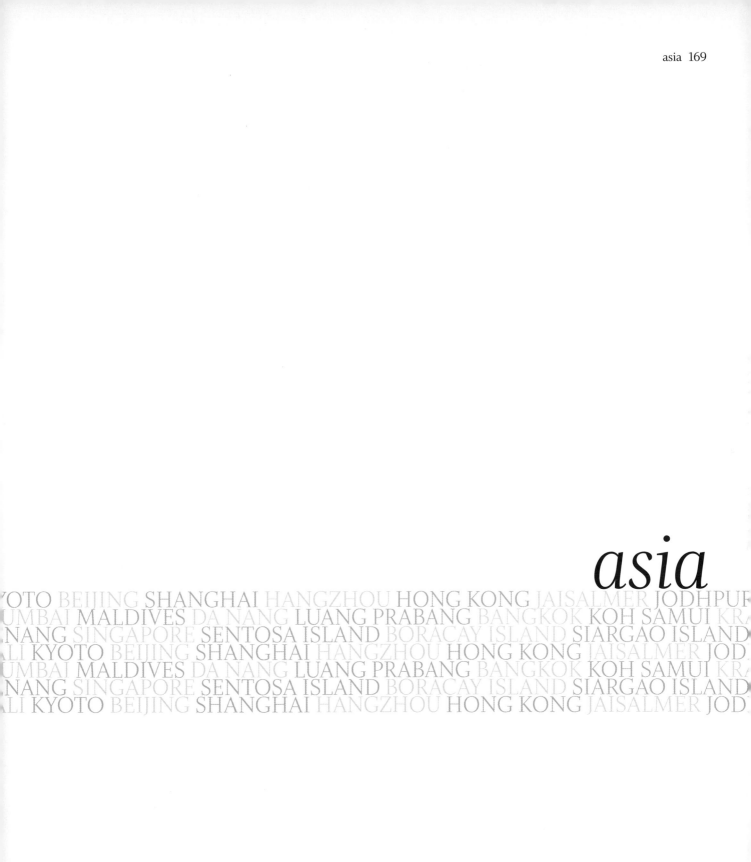

HOSHINOYA KYOTO

Kyoto, Japan

IN A FORESTED RIVER GORGE, KYOTO'S ARASHIYAMA NEIGHBORHOOD has offered a tranquil break from the urban din for a thousand years, a legacy that this *ryokan* has fully embraced. Accessible only via a 10- to 15-minute boat ride that departs from centuries-old Togetsukyo Bridge, the 25 guest rooms are housed within a series of historic buildings gently terraced along the riverbank. Each melds traditional teahouse-style architecture with a few well-chosen furnishings: a Japanese futon; a yellow cedar bathtub; hand-printed *washi*-paper screens. The artful restraint and meticulous attention to detail are echoed in the inn's food, composed of seasonal, regional ingredients—exquisitely marbled Wagyu beef, or bamboo shoots and scallops served with a sansho pepper–leaf dressing. In the morning, a *nabe* hot-pot breakfast is delivered to your room, where a backdrop of maple and cherry trees encourages Zen-like reflection. *11-2 Genrokuzan-cho, Arashiyama, Nishikyo-ku; 81-75/871-0001; kyoto.hoshinoya.com; doubles from $$$$$.*

Guest rooms overlooking the Ooigawa River at Hoshinoya Kyoto.

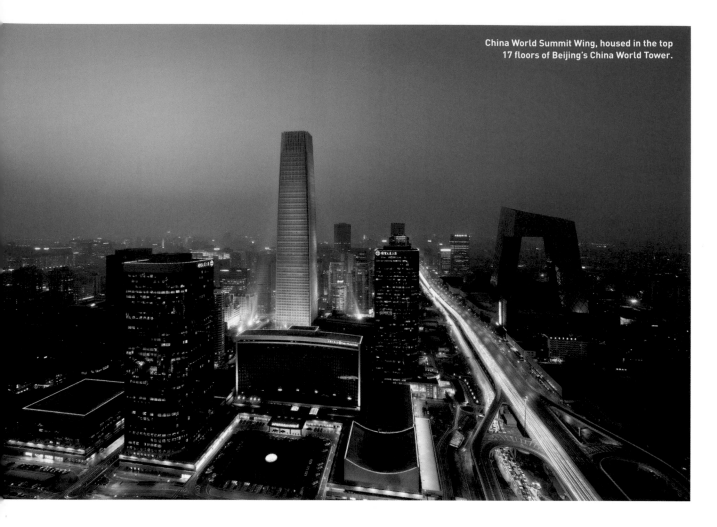

China World Summit Wing, housed in the top 17 floors of Beijing's China World Tower.

CHINA WORLD SUMMIT WING

Beijing

INTERNATIONAL CONVENTIONS AND A HIGH-END MALL make the China World Trade Center a popular hub for both business and leisure travelers. Now they have another place to spend the night: Shangri-La's China World Summit Wing, which occupies the top 17 floors of an 81-story skyscraper in the complex. The 278 guest rooms—which, starting at 700 square feet, are the largest in town—look down on the CCTV tower and the Forbidden City. An excellent Chi spa and an indoor infinity pool join a top-notch business center with around-the-clock secretarial, courier, and translation services. At Atmosphere, China's highest bar, mixologist Serhan Kusaksizoglu (known as Charlie) will ply you with his premium cache of bourbons, rye whiskeys, and single malts. Dining options include an outpost of Hong Kong's legendary restaurant Fook Lam Moon and a branch of Japan's kaiseki favorite Nadaman; CEO's, however, may prefer to broker their deals over a bespoke banquet in one of the hotel's two private dining rooms, both designed by Adam D. Tihany.

1 Jianguomenwai Ave., Central Business District; 866/565-5050 or 86-10/6505-2299; shangri-la.com; doubles from $$.

A Deluxe Suite at PuLi Hotel & Spa.

PULI HOTEL & SPA

Shanghai

EVEN IN THE HEART OF CHINA'S BUSIEST METROPOLIS, PuLi Hotel delivers a surprisingly serene experience. Imposing entry doors and a thriving grove of bamboo signal an immediate departure from the city bustle. A library with soaring ceilings and ebony-stained woodwork lies just off the lobby. In the 229 guest rooms, sliding silk screens delineate bedroom and bath spaces. All the expected high-tech amenities (iPod docking stations; sleek espresso machines) are complemented by traditional Chinese decorative elements, including brass incense burners, inkstone-topped tables, and protective timber foo dogs. The coup de grâce is the hotel's third floor, where an infinity-edge lap pool lined in glittering mosaic tiles overlooks Jing An Park, and the 5,380-square-foot Anantara Spa offers a menu of restorative treatments—from a purifying green-tea scrub to a bath scented with bergamot and peppermint oils. If all this relaxation has you feeling a little restless, stop by the lobby's 105-foot-long bar, one of the buzziest cocktail spots in town.
1 Changde Rd., Jing An; 86-21/3203-9999; thepuli.com; doubles from $$$.

spotlight hangzhou, china

EIGHT CENTURIES AGO, MARCO POLO ANOINTED HANGZHOU "THE MOST SPLENDID CITY IN THE WORLD." Today it's one of China's best-preserved destinations, thanks to the careful stewardship of its pagodas, mountain-fringed West Lake, and terraced green-tea plantations. More recently, three new world-class hotels have combined modern embellishments with inspiration from the city's timeless beauty. The 42 rooms at Amanfayun, the second property in China from Amanresorts, are arranged in brick-and-timber courtyard dwellings. Start your day with a soak in a deep Japanese-style tub, then go for a walk to the neighboring Lingyin Buddhist temple. A 25-minute drive away, Banyan Tree Hangzhou abuts the 2,800-acre Xixi National

Monks gathering in a courtyard outside Amanfayun.

AMANFAYUN

22 Fayun Nong, West Lake Scenic Area; 800/477-9180; amanresorts.com; doubles from $$$.

BANYAN TREE HANGZHOU

21 Zijingang Rd.; 800/591-0439; banyantree.com; doubles from $$$.

Wetland Park. All 72 suites and villas are decorated with Chinese antiques (porcelain snuff bottles; calligraphy brushes) and positioned around the grounds like a true village, complete with arched bridges and a lagoon. The city's most recent addition, the Four Seasons Hotel Hangzhou at West Lake, features painterly landscapes and a picturesque pond that make the property feel frozen in time. Look closer, however, and amid the hand-painted silk and wood wall panels in the 78 guest rooms you'll find techy touches, such as DVD players and LCD TV's. The Chinese-style gardens provide the ideal setting to sit for a spell over a cup of the region's *longjin* tea.

A living room inside one of Banyan Tree Hangzhou's villas.

The pavilion and gardens at Four Seasons Hotel Hangzhou at West Lake.

FOUR SEASONS HOTEL HANGZHOU AT WEST LAKE

5 Lingyin Rd.; 800/332-3442; fourseasons.com; doubles from $$.

The view from the Upper House's Studio 80.

UPPER HOUSE

Hong Kong

THE MOOD AT THIS MINIMALIST HOTEL is more like that of a pied-à-terre than a bustling big-city property. But there's nothing pared-down about the size of the Upper House's 117 rooms (the smallest is 730 square feet) or the quality of their materials: limestone bathrooms, shoji glass, glistening pale wood, and lacquered paper panels. Because rooms start at floor 38, there's hardly a bad view to be had—enjoy the vantage point from a custom L-shaped couch, or take in the Hong Kong skyline while soaking in a freestanding tub. Public spaces include a sixth-floor garden, where you can lounge on a bean bag or sprawl out on a grassy lawn, and the firelit 49th-floor Sky Lounge, which looks out on verdant Victoria Peak and the harbor. On the same level, a restaurant by star chef Gray Kunz serves up such dishes as seared tiger-prawn salad and snapper with green curry. Back in your room, consult your personal iPod Touch, loaded with music, games, and local tips. The hotel's two Lexus hybrids will take you wherever you want to go.
Pacific Place, 88 Queensway; 852/3968-1111; upperhouse. com; doubles from $$.

Sundecks in the Serai, Jaisalmer's pool area.

SERAI, JAISALMER

Jaisalmer, India

FANS OF THE LUXURY-TENT VACATION, TAKE NOTE: the Serai, Jaisalmer has raised the bar. Rajasthan's most lavish tented camp to date consists of 21 canvas structures that rest on smooth stone foundations and come with their own verandas (seven have private plunge pools). The campaign-style furnishings in each recall British military lodgings from the 1800's, albeit with a glamorous twist. If the epic landscape—the resort resides on 100 acres in the Thar Desert—doesn't clear your mind, a massage at the spa will. Embark on a guided tour of the golden fort and *haveli* residences of the walled city of Jaisalmer, 45 minutes away, or a camel safari in search of blackbuck and chinkara. At night, take a dip in the resort's infinity pool, modeled on a traditional Indian step well and lit by lanterns.
Bherwa, Chandan; 91-11/4617-2700; sujanluxury.com; doubles from $$$.

An aerial view of Jodhpur's Mihir Garh.

MIHIR GARH

Jodhpur, India

ON A SANDY DUNE IN THE WILD RAJASTHANI PLAINS, this palatial fortress provides a breathtaking respite from the energetic scene in Jodhpur, an hour to the north. Constructed in 2009 with crenellated ramparts that give it an imposing air, Mihir Garh is owned by one of the country's avid horsemen and features a stable of indigenous Marwari steeds; take one on a maharajah-style journey through the desert or on a guided picnic safari to a Bishnoi tribal village. Each of the nine suites (most over 1,700 square feet) are done up in rich textiles and furnishings carved from exotic woods, with modern-day comforts like plasma TV's, air-conditioning, and Jacuzzi tubs or plunge pools. After a day of exploring the surroundings, they're the perfect ending to a fairy-tale adventure.

Khandi, Rohet, Pali; 91-2936/268-231 or 91-291/243-1161; mihirgarh.com; doubles from $$$, including meals.

The contemporary lobby of the Oberoi, Mumbai, with its cherry-red Ritmüller piano.

OBEROI, MUMBAI

Mumbai

TEMPORARILY SHUTTERED AFTER THE TERRORIST ATTACKS in 2008, the Oberoi has been completely transformed, thanks to a $45 million refurbishment. The original exterior remains intact: a striking tower and adjacent cubelike structure set on the harbor in the heart of the commercial district. Inside, however, the changes are apparent. The atrium lobby, where waiters serve tea and cocktails, features white Thassos marble floors and black granite columns set off by vibrant red accents. The 287 guest rooms, decorated in an eye-catching palette of ivory, crimson, yellow, and sage, are roomier than ever and come equipped with Wi-Fi and iPod docking stations. Fighting off jet lag? The 24-hour spa has an array of restorative treatments, such as a coconut-milk scrub and an ayurvedic massage. Of course, increased security measures are found throughout the hotel, including a well-monitored entryway and dozens of discreetly placed cameras. But the overall effect is chic and smart—a longtime power brokers' hub that has stepped up its game.
Nariman Point; 800/562-3764 or 91-22/6632-5757; oberoihotels.com; doubles from $$$.

Golden Dragon restaurant at the Taj Mahal Palace. Left: Corridors in the Palace wing.

TAJ MAHAL PALACE

Mumbai

FROM ITS COMMANDING SPOT ON THE ARABIAN SEA, overlooking the 85-foot-high Gateway of India, the Taj Mahal Palace has been one of the country's premier properties for more than a century. The hotel was also targeted during the 2008 terrorist attacks and suffered damage that forced the Palace wing's closure. Now, after an intensive restoration, the wing has reopened, its grand public spaces featuring crystal chandeliers, hand-woven silk carpets, and onyx columns. The 285 rooms and suites maintain their classic aesthetic, with Edwardian furniture and original art, while the 275 accommodations in the Tower wing (popular with business travelers) are streamlined and contemporary. Frescoed constellations cover the ceiling of the Zodiac Grill, and the clubby Harbour Bar—now serving an international tapas menu—is still the watering hole of choice, as it has been since 1933.

Apollo Bunder; 866/969-1825 or 91-22/6665-3366; tajhotels.com; doubles from $$$.

SHANGRI-LA'S VILLINGILI RESORT & SPA

Addu Atoll, Maldives

ON A SANDY OUTCROPPING NEAR A CORAL REEF, Shangri-La has built a seaside retreat where visitors never lack for options. The 142 villas come with open-air showers and soaking tubs; choose one located right on the beach perched on stilts over the lagoon, or a treetop aerie equipped with its own infinity pool. Staffers see to your every request, whether you crave a private dinner underneath the coconut palms or a sunset ride on the resort's wooden yacht. In the spa, find your center with workshops on yoga and meditation and treatments tailored to your individual yin/yang. Then don your snorkel gear and follow the underwater signs on a submerged nature trail, or borrow a bicycle to cruise along the 10-mile road that connects Addu Atoll to five neighboring islands seemingly untouched by modern times. *Villingili Island; 866/565-5050 or 011-960/689-7888; shangri-la.com; doubles from $$$$$.*

A pool staff member at Shangri-La's Villingili Resort. Opposite: A water villa on the lagoon.

Furama Resort's freshwater lagoon pool. Opposite: Cushioned deck chairs.

FURAMA RESORT

Da Nang, Vietnam

IT'S HARD TO IMAGINE A MORE PICTURESQUE SPOT for an affordable resort than Bac My An, part of the 18-mile stretch of coastline in central Vietnam known to Americans as China Beach. Combining French colonial–era and traditional Vietnamese design, the 198 rooms at Furama exude a languid air, with plantation-style shutters and polished timber floors. But five restaurants and bars ensure the atmosphere is anything but sleepy. The hotel tends to attract adventurous types, thanks to an on-site water-sports center that arranges windsurfing, ocean kayaking, and Jet Ski excursions, as well as diving expeditions along the Son Tra Peninsula to see corals and other subtropical sea life. And there's no shortage of cultural diversions: four UNESCO World Heritage sites are within driving distance, including Hoi An's ancient pagodas and the Phong Nha Caves, a subterranean system of passageways in Vietnam's largest primeval jungle.

68 Ho Xuan Huong St., Bac My An; 800/223-5652 or 84-511/384-7888; furamavietnam.com; doubles from $, including breakfast.

AMANTAKA

Luang Prabang, Laos

LONG IN THE SHADOWS OF THAILAND'S CHIANG MAI, LUANG PRABANG IS THAT RARE PLACE IN ASIA—a calm and somnolent city. Its narrow lanes, timber houses, and markets are set along a peninsular thumb in the Mekong River, surrounded by mountains that have helped guard against overdevelopment. Marking its transition to high-end destination, Amanresorts' Amantaka incorporates a UNESCO-protected former French hospital. Its 24 suites feature four-poster beds, freestanding bathtubs, and louvered doors that open onto patios shaded by mango trees. A library and art gallery provide plenty of cultural enrichment, but visitors are encouraged to venture out to the 32 temples nearby—active centers of worship and learning, with saffron-robed monks who serve as the town's animating force.
55/53 Kingkitsarath Rd., Ban Thongchaleun; 800/477-9180 or 856-71/860-333; amanresorts.com; doubles from $$$, including airport transfers.

The entrance to
Amantaka resort's
fitness facility. Opposite:
The swimming pool.

A Scenic City room at Navalai River Resort. Left: Aquatini restaurant, overlooking the Chao Phraya River.

NAVALAI RIVER RESORT

Bangkok

ON THE BANKS OF THE CHAO PHRAYA RIVER, five minutes from the bars and cafés of Bangkok's pulsing Khao San Road, this 74-room boutique hotel delivers on location, style, and—the ultimate 21st-century luxury—space. The Navalai River Resort blends traditional Thai architecture with streamlined modern touches: the Artist suites feature works from contemporary photographers and 1960's-inspired furniture, while the Rattanakosin Heritage rooms have ornate headboards and regal gold and white accents. Splurge on a River Breeze room (the larger balcony is worth the extra baht), then spend an afternoon lounging at the blue-tiled rooftop pool after a therapeutic massage at the spa. The ferry stop at the hotel's back doorstep makes day-trips to the nearby Emerald Buddha and Marble Temple almost effortless.
45/1-2 Phra Athit Rd., Phra Nakorn; 66-2/280-9955; navalai.com; doubles from $, including breakfast.

Langham Place Samui, as seen from an ocean dock. Left: A Pavilion Pool villa.

LANGHAM PLACE SAMUI AT LAMAI BEACH

Koh Samui, Thailand

AIMED AT TRAVELERS WHO REQUIRE A WI-FI CONNECTION with their R&R, the 77-room Langham Place Samui promises to keep you plugged-in everywhere on the property, from your villa's canopy bed to the powder-soft sand. The resort sits on the outskirts of Koh Samui's trendy Lamai Beach, with shopping and nightlife just a short walk away; a catwalk-like entry runs between granite-walled waterfalls into the lobby lounge, where a DJ spins down-tempo beats nightly. That's not to say the hotel doesn't inspire relaxation. Interiors are done in a soothing palette of cream and taupe silks and dark wood, and in seven Ocean-View Pool Villas, the oversize tubs in the bathrooms are open to the elements. A sunbathing deck extends from the 650-foot-long dock beyond the beachfront pool. Each evening, Thai paper lanterns are released into the sky, a symbol of your everyday cares floating away.

146/24 Moo 4, Lamai Beach; 800/588-9141 or 66-77/960-888; langhamhotels.com; doubles from $, including breakfast.

PHULAY BAY, A RITZ-CARLTON RESERVE

Krabi, Thailand

EXPECTATIONS WERE HIGH FOR RITZ-CARLTON'S NEW, CULTURALLY CONSCIOUS RESERVE BRAND—and its first property in Krabi, Phuket's unspoiled neighbor, more than delivers. Bangkok-based architect and interior designer Lek Bunnag skillfully worked indigenous motifs—frescoes painted by northern Thai artists; enormous *mai sak* (teakwood) doors; a pitched-roof pavilion seemingly suspended above a reflecting pool—throughout the resort's contemporary setting. The 54 villas and suites, some of which come with outdoor baths and private plunge pools, are each assigned a personal butler who can arrange excursions by longtail boat to nearby Hong Island or Thai cooking classes with a master chef. Come sunset, settle into one of the daybeds at the open-air Chomtawan lounge with a signature Phulatini cocktail in hand and the Andaman Sea as far as the eye can see.

111 Moo 3, Tamboon Nongthalay, Amphur Muang; 800/542-8680 or 66-75/628-111; ritzcarlton.com; doubles from $$$$$.

Phulay Bay's infinity pool, overlooking the Andaman Sea. Opposite: A lounge in the resort's spa.

The swimming pool at Clove Hall. Opposite, from left: Bottled water in a guest room; the private veranda outside the Star Anise suite.

CLOVE HALL

Penang, Malaysia

PENANG'S BRITISH PORT OF GEORGE TOWN WAS GRANTED WORLD HERITAGE STATUS in the summer of 2008. Since then, it has experienced a renaissance, its colonial buildings reinvented as galleries, cafés, and hotels—including Clove Hall, a six-room property amid tropical gardens on a former coconut plantation. Hotelier Christopher Ong, known for restoring former residences such as Sri Lanka's Galle Fort Hotel, rehabilitated the 1910 Edwardian mansion into a gracious retreat wrapped in colonnaded verandas and shaded by ginger and palm trees. Rooms are filled with antiques from Ong's personal collection: teak four-poster beds, cane chairs, and mahogany rolltop desks. Book a tasting menu of traditional Nyonya (Malay-spiked Chinese) cuisine in the inn's dining room, its tables set with delicate blue-and-white-patterned porcelain dishes, or take to the streets to check out the thriving restaurant scene just steps away.
11 Clove Hall Rd.; 011-604/229-0818; clovehall.com; doubles from $.

194

The Marina Bay Sands Hotel at dusk.

MARINA BAY SANDS HOTEL

Singapore

A BUDGET THE SIZE OF SOUTH CAROLINA'S. A PARK SUSPENDED 650 FEET in the air. More than 7,000 employees. Singapore's $5.5 billion Marina Bay Sands is set to catapult the tiny island country near Malaysia into the ranks of futuristic, vertigo-inducing cities like Dubai. Designed by Moshe Safdie, the hotel is a mini-city composed of three curving towers that house a staggering 2,561 guest rooms. Landscaped gardens, a nearly 500-foot-long infinity pool, and an observation deck rest on a three-acre surfboard-shaped platform atop the three structures, overlooking the South China Sea, Marina Bay, and the Singapore skyline. Seven restaurants include outposts from some of the food world's most famous names—Daniel Boulud, Guy Savoy, and Tetsuya Wakuda. After dark, try your luck in the atrium casino, where the chandelier is made of 132,000 Swarovski crystals, then head to one of the resort's three club lounges, two of which float on pavilions in the bay. It's a fittingly glitzy end to a day in Asia's eye-popping new playground.
10 Bayfront Ave.; 65/6688-8868; marinabaysands.com; doubles from $$.

Rooms at Capella Singapore display art from the hotel's growing collection. Right: The 19th-century main buildings.

CAPELLA SINGAPORE

Sentosa Island, Singapore

IT'S NO WONDER THAT CAPELLA CHOSE THE RECENTLY REVITALIZED SENTOSA for its Asian debut. Known for its placid beaches and golf courses, the island off Singapore's southern coast already had seven comfortable hotels, but none with this combination of colonial grace and modern architecture. Two columned buildings dating from the 1880's, with red-tile roofs and wide verandas, are surrounded by a curvaceous glass-and-steel structure designed by Foster & Partners. Cane chairs and teak woodwork are classic touches amid the contemporary interiors (ask for one of the top-floor corner Constellation rooms, which follow the building's arc and have semicircular bedrooms and gently rounded balconies). In the spa, signature treatments based on the lunar cycle draw on Singapore's Malay and Chinese traditions. Don't miss the weekend dim sum brunch at Cassia, whose alfresco dining area looks out over green gardens and colonial manors.
1 The Knolls; 877/247-6688 or 65/6591-5018; capellasingapore.com; doubles from $$$.

A pool villa master bedroom at Shangri-La's Boracay Resort.

SHANGRI-LA'S BORACAY RESORT & SPA

Boracay Island, Philippines

A LONGTIME BACKPACKER HAVEN 200 MILES SOUTH OF MANILA, Boracay finally has a five-star property worthy of its white-sand coastline. Situated along a sheltered cove within an eco-reserve, the 219 rooms and villas are filled with indigenous touches and natural materials, from woven abaca rugs and capiz shell lamps to balconies crafted from hardwoods. For an especially memorable stay, snag the vertiginous Tree Top Villa, which has a whirlpool and some of the property's best vistas of the azure Sulu Sea. Families are clearly welcome and well catered to: a series of Day-Glo-colored spaces house a bank of foosball and air hockey tables and private karaoke rooms. After a trip to one of the more than 20 dive sites along nearby Punta Bunga and Bunyugan reefs, unwind with a drink at the cliff-top Solana Bar, built on a series of open-air platforms. *Barangay Yapak; 866/565-5050 or 63-36/288-4988; shangri-la.com; doubles from $$.*

Kalinaw Resort's infinity pool, overlooking a lagoon.

KALINAW RESORT

Siargao Island, Philippines

A LEGENDARY SURF BREAK BROUGHT GLOBE-TROTTING PARISIANS Fred Debacker and Pierre Zappavigna to Siargao Island in 2005. Once there, the two designers decided to forsake big-city life and open Kalinaw Resort, which means "peaceful" in the native Visayan dialect. The intimate hideaway blends a laid-back, beach-friendly atmosphere and high-end design, appealing to surf bums and urbanites alike. Locally sourced nipa leaves and dark *doyok-doyok*–wood floors set off the minimalist furnishings (platform beds shrouded in white linens) in the five airy lagoon-side villas. The owners, both infectiously enthusiastic about their adopted home, are eager to suggest excursions during your stay. Among the options: Magpupungko Pool, a crystal-clear natural swimming hole enclosed by fantastic rock formations, and a trimaran tour of the white-sand islets that surround the resort. But be sure to grab a surfboard and try your own luck on the barrel-shaped wave, known as Cloud 9, that drew Debacker and Zappavigna here in the first place. *General Luna; 63-921/320-0442; kalinawresort.com; doubles from $, including breakfast.*

A private pool cabana at Alila Villas Uluwatu.
Opposite, from top: Inside the Warung; king prawns
with black rice risotto, served at Cire restaurant.

ALILA VILLAS ULUWATU

Bali, Indonesia

BALI'S MOST SEDUCTIVE NEW GETAWAY HAS ONE FOOT IN THE AIR (an impossibly cantilevered pavilion that seems to float skyward over a cliff) and the other firmly planted in the earth. Built in accordance with Green Globe principles, the resort recycles its water and uses sustainable materials, including bamboo and lava stone from the island and wood from neighboring Java. In each of the 84 villas, a bedroom wall opens onto a frangipani-shaded pool and pavilion, with the Indian Ocean in the distance. The resort lies on the southern coast of the Bukit Peninsula, a quiet corner known for surfing and temples—take a tour with a knowledgeable guide, just one of the immersive cultural forays the hotel offers. Another transcendent experience: a meal at the Warung, the Alila's Indonesian restaurant, whose tongue-tingling *soto ayam* (a Balinese spiced chicken noodle soup) is the best dish you'll have on your entire trip.
Jalan Belimbing Sari, Banjar Tambiyak, Desa Pecatu; 800/337-4685 or 62-361/848-2166; alilahotels.com; doubles from $$$, including daily wellness classes.

The patio at Black Barn Retreats, in New Zealand's Havelock North.

australia, new zealand & the south pacific

SMANIA ROTTNEST ISLAND BROOME LITHGOW SYDNEY YERING SORREN
VELOCK NORTH AKAROA FIJI TASMANIA ROTTNEST ISLAND BROOME LI
DNEY YERING SORRENTO HAVELOCK NORTH AKAROA FIJI TASMANIA RO
AND BROOME LITHGOW SYDNEY YERING SORRENTO HAVELOCK NORTH
I TASMANIA ROTTNEST ISLAND BROOME LITHGOW SYDNEY YERING SOR
VELOCK NORTH AKAROA FIJI TASMANIA ROTTNEST ISLAND BROOME LIT
DNEY YERING SORRENTO HAVELOCK NORTH AKAROA FIJI TASMANIA RO

spotlight *tasmania*

UNTIL RECENTLY, TASMANIA'S CHOICE OF LODGINGS—mostly basic motels or folksy bed-and-breakfasts—meant that visiting the heart-shaped island was, by default, a less than upmarket affair. Thankfully, more indulgent accommodations are raising the level of the travel experience in Australia's smallest and most isolated state. Near the Tamar Valley, the Quamby Estate was once the centerpiece of an 1830's farm owned by Tasmania's first native-born premier. The sprawling homestead has been converted into 10 spacious rooms with flagstone verandas, timber shutters, and views of serene English gardens; the staff can arrange seasonal truffle hunts and tours of surrounding wineries. At Saffire Freycinet, an architecturally striking resort on a

A Deluxe room at Quamby Estate.

The Hazards Mountains, as seen from Saffire Freycinet's main entrance.

QUAMBY ESTATE

1145 Westwood Rd., Hagley; 61-3/6392-2211; quambyestate.com; doubles from $$, including breakfast.

SAFFIRE FREYCINET

2352 Coles Bay Rd., Coles Bay; 61-3/6256-7888; saffire-freycinet.com.au; doubles from $$$$$, all-inclusive.

wildlife-rich peninsula off the eastern coast, floor-to-ceiling glass walls overlook the cobalt waters of Great Oyster Bay. Chef Hugh Whitehouse's food-immersion programs take you directly to the source—tag along with him to nearby Freycinet Marine Farm to harvest Pacific oysters, or sign up for a hands-on rock-lobster cooking class taught right in your Premium suite. On the northwestern coast, in the 19th-century settlement of Stanley, the boutique hotel @VDLStanley consists of three high-ceilinged, stone-walled suites in an 1843 commercial warehouse built from the ballast of English ships. That plateau-like mass of volcanic rock out your window? That's the Nut, Tasmania's own version of South Africa's Table Mountain.

The stone exterior of @VDLStanley.

@VDLSTANLEY

16 Wharf Rd., Stanley; 61-3/6458-2032; atvdlstanley.com.au; doubles from $.

Bike riding on the boardwalk along Thomson Bay.

HOTEL ROTTNEST

Rottnest Island, Australia

WHEN DUTCH MARINERS FIRST ARRIVED AT THIS BEACH-RINGED landmass in 1658, it was the sight of the rare quokka—a marsupial that they mistook for a rodent—that prompted them to dub the island Rottnest ("rat's nest"). Since those unprepossessing beginnings, the sun-drenched, car-free reserve and its kangaroo-like inhabitants have become a popular draw for day-trippers from Perth, an easy ferry ride away. There are very few places to spend the night, and that's how the locals like it; the best is the Hotel Rottnest, which was built in the 1860's as a governor's mansion. After a two-year renovation, its architecture remains intact, but the 18 rooms have been refreshed with minimalist comforts: charcoal-hued rattan chairs and angular furnishings set off by spare white walls. Located on Thomson Bay, the hotel is known for its stellar views and happening bar scene. Fuel up on king prawns and Coffin Bay oysters, then cycle down to the Wadjemup Lighthouse, a limestone tower that affords a timeless photo op. *1 Bedford Ave.; 61-8/9292-5011; hotelrottnest.com.au; doubles from $$.*

Rock formations along the coast of the Indian Ocean at Eco Beach.

ECO BEACH WILDERNESS RETREAT

Broome, Australia

IT'S ONLY ABOUT AN HOUR FROM THE FAST-GROWING TOWN OF Broome, but Eco Beach Wilderness Retreat has the feel of a much more remote destination. Set along an empty stretch of the Indian Ocean in Western Australia, with views of red rock formations that give the landscape an almost lunar-like beauty, the 25 beachside villas and 30 tents are sprinkled among eucalyptus groves and positioned to catch breezes off the water. But the resort's most striking feature is its unswerving devotion to sustainability without scrimping on creature comforts. Rooftop solar panels power reading lamps, ceiling fans, and air conditioners, and in-room controls allow guests to monitor their energy usage. At the oceanfront Jack's Bar & Grill, inventive Asian-Aussie cuisine—grilled barramundi with parsley and lemon; duck, pea, and pumpkin samosas—is made with herbs and produce plucked from the property's gardens. Given the pristine environment, the area is a wonderland of nature activities. Explore the caves and surrounding bush, go on a guided trek and learn to gather food with the native Yawuru people, or hike to the cliff-top Dampier Lookout, which provides the perfect perch for spotting dolphins and, from July through September, migrating whales. *Lot 323 Dampier Location, Great Northern Hwy.; 61-8/9193-8015; ecobeach.com.au; doubles from $.*

Wolgan Valley Resort's 1832 Heritage Homestead.

WOLGAN VALLEY RESORT & SPA

Lithgow, Australia

FOR THOSE WHO EQUATE ECO-FRIENDLY PRINCIPLES WITH A CRUNCHY, back-to-the-land aesthetic, Australia's first luxury conservation-based resort comes as a welcome surprise. The 4,000-acre Wolgan Valley fits harmoniously into a craggy Grand Canyon–like setting three hours west of Sydney, providing guests with the first serious safari experience down under. Set within its own nature reserve, the property offers daily wildlife drives in search of kangaroos and wallabies; field guides are on hand to lead other activities, from a horseback ride across the plains to a mountain-bike excursion along the edge of a freshwater dam. After a day of outback adventure, afternoon tea and scones await, along with considerable comforts: the 40 freestanding suites have indoor-outdoor plunge pools, double-sided fireplaces, and verandas. In keeping with the environmentally conscious ethos, the furniture is locally made, and the bathroom toiletries are biodegradable. Five-course dinners are served in the timber and sandstone Main Homestead, which is inspired by the country's pioneer architecture. *2600 Wolgan Rd.; 61-2/9290-9733; wolganvalley.com; doubles from $$$$$, all-inclusive.*

A penthouse loft at Establishment Hotel.

ESTABLISHMENT HOTEL

Sydney

PART OUTSIZE BEACH RESORT, PART CULTURE CAPITAL, Sydney exemplifies the art of relaxed urbanity: stylish but not pretentious, cutting-edge without being aggressively hip. A stone's throw from Circular Quay and the Opera House, the Establishment Hotel—housed within a mini-complex that includes several bars and nightlife venues—channels that inimitable Aussie energy. The low-lit lobby makes for an alluring introduction to the 31 rooms, where Modernist furnishings are cloaked in a palette of gray, white, and dark pink and set off by floors of Japanese timber. Bathrooms have granite tubs and double-sink vanities, along with rain showers and Bulgari amenities; temperature and lighting are controlled from a touch-screen console. Given its location, the Establishment is understandably popular with the late-night set. The celebs you spot are most likely en route to the perennially packed Hemmesphere lounge, one of Sydney's most exclusive clubs—only an elevator ride away.
5 Bridge St.; 61-2/9240-3000; establishmenthotel.com; doubles from $$.

CHATEAU YERING HOTEL

Yering, Australia

KNOWN FOR ITS GENTLY ROLLING LANDSCAPES AND HIGHLY democratized wine scene, obscure Yarra Valley couldn't be further from the glitz of California's Napa. An hour northeast of Melbourne's airport, the region has no major architectural achievements, tour buses, or rarefied bottlings that inspire cultish devotion among vino geeks—just a collection of down-to-earth wineries, including Chateau Yering. Built on the area's first vineyard and flanked by English-style gardens, the restored mansion calls to mind the valley's Victorian beginnings with pale blue walls, velvet drapes, and Australian cedar doors and window jambs dating from 1854. The 32 suites range from genteel (antique furniture; claw-foot tubs) to lodgelike (crackling fireplaces; red plaid fabrics; wraparound decks). At Eleonore's, the hotel's fine-dining restaurant, guests can feast on milk-fed Yeringberg lamb accompanied by a bottle or two from the 250-acre estate. They're best tasted, of course, in true Yarra Valley fashion: with appreciation, but without the slightest hint of wine snobbery. *42 Melba Hwy.; 61-3/9237-3333; chateauyering.com.au; doubles from $$$.*

Chateau Yering, nestled in the Yarra Valley. Opposite: A stone path outside the drawing room.

HOTEL SORRENTO

Sorrento, Victoria, Australia

ON FRIDAY AFTERNOONS FROM DECEMBER THROUGH FEBRUARY, THE peak of Australian summer, Melbourne natives pack their bags and head straight for the beach town of Sorrento, 1½ hours south of Melbourne on the far western tip of the Mornington Peninsula. In an 1872 building high on a cliff above the small harbor, the family-run Hotel Sorrento retains its historic charm—witness the solid, locally quarried limestone walls—despite the addition of newer structures that house units with gas fireplaces and full kitchens. (Ask for one of the On the Hill apartments for balcony views of bottlenose dolphins swimming past Port Phillip Bay.) The lively Limeburners Bar, named for the generations of laborers who fired lime in kilns to create the stone, is another nod to Sorrento tradition. The hotel makes an excellent base for a laid-back Australian escape; your day might consist of surfing in the morning, a languid lunch in town, and fish-and-chips on the beach at sunset. *5-15 Hotham Rd.; 61-3/5984-8000; hotelsorrento.com.au; doubles from $$, including breakfast.*

One of the Heritage suites at Hotel Sorrento.

Inside a River Lodge at Black Barn Retreats. Opposite, from top: Chocolate crème brûlée from the Bistro; Bronwynne Thorpe.

BLACK BARN RETREATS

Havelock North, New Zealand

FAMED FOR ITS CHARDONNAYS, Sauvignon Blancs, and Bordeaux-style reds, Black Barn Vineyards is many things besides a winery: summer concert venue, modern art gallery, and restaurant. It's also home to one of the most appealing lodging options in the pastoral wine region of Hawkes Bay. Thirteen bungalows—plus a six-bedroom house with a tennis court—are dotted around the hamlet of Havelock North and overseen in highly personal good taste by owner Kim Thorp and his wife, Bronwynne. Overstuffed sofas sit next to river-rock fireplaces and picture windows looking out onto the Tukituki River; two more cabins are nestled among almond, olive, and citrus trees on the vineyard proper. The owners' reverence for *terroir* is evident at every turn. Seasonal dishes are served beneath a vine-shaded pergola at the Bistro, and a farmers' market is held weekly during the summer. Attendants at an informal concierge desk within the winery building point guests to hidden surf spots and the area's best farmstead cheese makers.
R12 Black Barn Rd.; 64-6/877-7985; blackbarn.com; cottages from $$.

Maison de la Mer's Provence Suite.
Left: The inn's kitchen, with organic,
free-range eggs from a farm nearby.

MAISON DE LA MER

Akaroa, New Zealand

THE TINY FORMER WHALING TOWN OF AKAROA can swell to the thousands during the summer, as Kiwis crowd the picturesque harbor in search of sand and cerulean sea. Thankfully, an intimate stay is guaranteed at the Maison de la Mer, a waterfront Arts and Crafts–style house in the middle of the village. In 2004, owners Carol and Bruce Hyland painstakingly restored the property, giving interiors a breezy French-country feel. Then they added the kind of thoughtful touches that make visitors feel more like friends, including Carol's fresh-out-of-the-oven Ricciarelli cookies, complimentary chocolates and port wine served nightly, and a library of DVD's. Choose from one of the three rooms in the main house or book the nautically inspired Boathouse suite, which comes with its own kitchen and balcony and a porthole window overlooking the harbor. The biggest incentive to rise early: Carol's bounteous breakfasts of local organic berries, house-made yogurt and muesli, and free-range eggs, served on her collection of fine china.

1 Rue Benoit; 64-3/304-8907; maisondelamer.co.nz; doubles from $$, including breakfast and in-suite snacks and beverages.

The Peninsula Residence on Laucala Island.

LAUCALA ISLAND

Fiji

BUSINESS TYCOON MALCOLM FORBES—a man well acquainted with the finer things—may have been the island's previous owner, but Austrian entrepreneur Dietrich Mateschitz, CEO of Red Bull, is the force behind this 3,000-acre getaway. Although its far-flung location—and price—practically guarantee an elite guest roster, Laucala's list of activities has all-inclusive appeal. At sea, there's game fishing, sailing, and diving the surrounding coral reef. On land, it's 18-hole golf, mountain biking, or cooking classes, not to mention three miles of rain forest trails to explore on horseback or foot. Guests arrive via private turboprop plane and are ushered to one of 25 villas crafted of mahogany and Fijian vesi woods, each with its own outdoor shower and pool. At the spa kitchen, you can create a custom blend of herbs to be used in a treatment tailored to your individual needs. The food served in the property's five restaurants is entirely local: fish is caught just offshore, cattle and poultry are raised on the island, and produce comes from a 240-acre farm nearby. It's self-sufficiency at its most glamorous. *011-679/888-0077; laucala.com; villas from $$$$$, all-inclusive.*

the world's best

In *Travel + Leisure*'s annual World's Best Awards Survey, readers are asked to rate their favorite hotels and spas around the globe, based on location, food, service, and value. Each year, the list of winners reveals readers' evolving, but always exacting, standards of excellence. You'll find the most recent results on the following pages, organized by region.

Nº3 WORLDWIDE HOTEL
FAIRMONT MARA SAFARI CLUB Masai Mara, Kenya

TOP 100 HOTELS

1. **OBEROI VANYAVILAS** Ranthambore, India 97.26
2. **TRIPLE CREEK RANCH** Darby, Montana 96.76
3. **FAIRMONT MARA SAFARI CLUB** Masai Mara, Kenya 96.31
4. **SAN YSIDRO RANCH, A ROSEWOOD RESORT**
   Santa Barbara, California 96.17
5. **OBEROI AMARVILAS** Agra, India 95.94
6. **NISBET PLANTATION BEACH CLUB** Nevis 95.75
7. **THE PENINSULA** Bangkok 95.69
8. **PALAZZO SASSO** Ravello, Italy 95.17
9. **DOMAINE DES HAUTS DE LOIRE** Onzain, France 95.00 $
9. **FOUR SEASONS HOTEL MÉXICO, D.F.** Mexico City 95.00
11. **JADE MOUNTAIN** St. Lucia 94.91
12. **LE SIRENUSE** Positano, Italy 94.88
13. **OBEROI RAJVILAS** Jaipur, India 94.78
14. **FOUR SEASONS HOTEL** Singapore 94.75
15. **OBEROI UDAIVILAS** Udaipur, India 94.71
16. **ROYAL MALEWANE** Kruger National Park, South Africa 94.67
16. **SINGITA SABI SAND (EBONY LODGE, BOULDERS LODGE, CASTLETON CAMP)** Sabi Sand Reserve, South Africa 94.67
18. **OLISSIPPO LAPA PALACE** Lisbon 94.60
19. **HÔTEL DE CRILLON** Paris 94.40
20. **SHANGRI-LA HOTEL** Singapore 94.32
20. **TRUMP INTERNATIONAL HOTEL & TOWER** Chicago 94.32 ⊙
22. **SINGITA KRUGER NATIONAL PARK (LEBOMBO LODGE, SWENI LODGE)** South Africa 94.25
23. **LONDOLOZI PRIVATE GAME RESERVE** Sabi Sand Reserve, South Africa 94.18
24. **TORTILIS CAMP, AMBOSELI** Kenya 94.12
24. **WOODLANDS RESORT & INN** Summerville, South Carolina 94.12
26. **THE PENINSULA** Hong Kong 94.11
27. **FOUR SEASONS RESORT** Chiang Mai, Thailand 93.95
28. **TAJ MAHAL PALACE** Mumbai 93.83
29. **HÔTEL DE LA PAIX** Siem Reap, Cambodia 93.75 ⊙
30. **&BEYOND KICHWA TEMBO MASAI MARA TENTED CAMP** Kenya 93.71
31. **FOUR SEASONS HOTEL** Dublin 93.68 $
32. **HOTEL BEL-AIR** (reopening in 2011) Los Angeles 93.67
33. **VILLA D'ESTE** Cernobbio, Italy 93.66
34. **TWELVE APOSTLES HOTEL & SPA** Cape Town 93.62

35. **RAMBAGH PALACE** Jaipur, India 93.60
36. **HOTEL SPLENDIDO** Portofino, Italy 93.52
37. **JAMAICA INN & SPA** Ocho Rios, Jamaica 93.50
38. **THE LANESBOROUGH, A ST. REGIS HOTEL** London 93.47
39. **TAJ LAKE PALACE** Udaipur, India 93.46
40. **STAFFORD LONDON** 93.44
41. **FOUR SEASONS RESORT JACKSON HOLE** Wyoming 93.43
41. **INN AT PALMETTO BLUFF** Bluffton, South Carolina 93.43
43. **HÔTEL CHÂTEAU EZA** Èze Village, France 93.33
44. **FOUR SEASONS HOTEL CAIRO AT THE FIRST RESIDENCE** 93.27
45. **MANDARIN ORIENTAL DHARA DHEVI** Chiang Mai, Thailand 93.26
46. **WICKANINNISH INN** Tofino, British Columbia 93.14
47. **POST RANCH INN** Big Sur, California 93.13
48. **THE PENINSULA** Chicago 93.09
49. **MALAMALA GAME RESERVE** South Africa 93.07
49. **POST HOTEL & SPA** Lake Louise, Alberta 93.07
51. **RITZ-CARLTON BEIJING, FINANCIAL STREET** 93.04
52. **LITTLE PALM ISLAND RESORT & SPA** Little Torch Key, Florida 92.97
52. **RITTENHOUSE HOTEL** Philadelphia 92.97
54. **FOUR SEASONS HOTEL GRESHAM PALACE** Budapest 92.96
55. **MANDARIN ORIENTAL** Prague 92.94 ⊙
56. **ESPERANZA, AN AUBERGE RESORT** Los Cabos, Mexico 92.91
57. **MANDARIN ORIENTAL** Bangkok 92.89
58. **THE PENINSULA** Beijing 92.88
59. **MANDARIN ORIENTAL** Hong Kong 92.84
60. **AUBERGE SAINT-ANTOINE** Quebec City 92.80

Throughout the World's Best Awards, scores are rounded
to the nearest hundredth of a point; in the event of a tie, properties
share the same ranking.

$ Denotes a Great Value (rate of $250 or less)
⊙ Denotes a debut on the World's Best Awards list

N°3 WORLDWIDE DESTINATION SPA
ENCHANTMENT RESORT & MII AMO SPA, Sedona, Arizona

TOP 100 HOTELS CONT.

61. **FOUR SEASONS HOTEL GEORGE V** Paris 92.76
62. **FOUR SEASONS RESORT HUALALAI** Hawaii 92.74
63. **BLANCANEAUX LODGE** San Ignacio, Belize 92.73
64. **CHÂTEAU DE LA CHÈVRE D'OR** Èze Village, France 92.71
65. **ONE&ONLY PALMILLA** Los Cabos, Mexico 92.69
66. **FOUR SEASONS HOTEL ISTANBUL AT SULTANAHMET** 92.63
67. **ROYAL LIVINGSTONE** Victoria Falls, Zambia 92.59
68. **SERENGETI SOPA LODGE** Tanzania 92.57
69. **CAPE GRACE** Cape Town 92.52
69. **SONNENALP RESORT OF VAIL** Colorado 92.52
71. **FEARRINGTON HOUSE COUNTRY INN** Pittsboro, North Carolina 92.47
72. **COUPLES TOWER ISLE** St. Mary, Jamaica 92.47
73. **HALEKULANI** Oahu 92.43
74. **FAIRMONT MOUNT KENYA SAFARI CLUB** Nanyuki, Kenya 92.29
75. **ROSEWOOD MANSION ON TURTLE CREEK** Dallas 92.28
76. **LEELA PALACE KEMPINSKI** Bengaluru (Bangalore), India 92.27
76. **SUTTON PLACE HOTEL** Chicago 92.27 ⑤ ❂
78. **ALVEAR PALACE HOTEL** Buenos Aires 92.25
79. **BAUR AU LAC** Zurich 92.20
80. **RITZ-CARLTON NEW YORK, CENTRAL PARK** 92.17
81. **MONTAGE LAGUNA BEACH** California 92.15
82. **PALACIO DUHAU-PARK HYATT** Buenos Aires 92.00
83. **THE PENINSULA** Beverly Hills 91.92
84. **FOUR SEASONS HOTEL** Hong Kong 91.86
85. **HOTEL VILLA SAN MICHELE** Fiesole, Italy 91.80

86. **LITTLE NELL** Aspen, Colorado 91.78
87. **FOUR SEASONS HOTEL** Chicago 91.77
88. **FOUR SEASONS HOTEL** Milan 91.77
89. **SOFITEL WASHINGTON D.C. LAFAYETTE SQUARE** 91.72
90. **LA COLOMBE D'OR HOTEL** St.-Paul-de-Vence, France 91.67
90. **MEADOWOOD NAPA VALLEY** St. Helena, California 91.67
92. **RITZ-CARLTON** Santiago, Chile 91.65
93. **AUBERGE DU SOLEIL** Rutherford, California 91.61
94. **BURJ AL ARAB** Dubai 91.57 ❂
95. **FOUR SEASONS RESORT** Carmelo, Uruguay 91.53
95. **KAHALA HOTEL & RESORT** Oahu 91.53
97. **HOTEL IMPERIAL, A LUXURY COLLECTION HOTEL** Vienna 91.52
98. **HOUSTONIAN HOTEL, CLUB & SPA** Houston 91.51 ❂
99. **THE LANGHAM** Melbourne 91.50 ⑤
100. **THE ADOLPHUS** Dallas 91.48 ⑤ ❂

TOP 10
DESTINATION SPAS

1. **RANCHO LA PUERTA** Tecate, Mexico 95.50
2. **CAL-A-VIE HEALTH SPA** Vista, California 92.27
3. **ENCHANTMENT RESORT & MII AMO SPA** Sedona, Arizona 91.86
4. **CANYON RANCH IN LENOX** Massachusetts 88.35
5. **CANYON RANCH IN TUCSON** Arizona 87.45
6. **REGENCY HEALTH RESORT & SPA** Hallandale, Florida 87.29
7. **MIRAVAL RESORT & SPA** Tucson, Arizona 87.15
8. **LAKE AUSTIN SPA RESORT** Austin, Texas 86.58
9. **CANYON RANCH HOTEL & SPA IN MIAMI BEACH** 86.33
10. **CHOPRA CENTER FOR WELLBEING** Carlsbad, California 86.29

N⁰2 WORLDWIDE DESTINATION SPA
CAL-A-VIE HEALTH SPA, Vista, California

Nº1 CONTINENTAL U.S. + CANADA **RESORT**
SAN YSIDRO RANCH, A ROSEWOOD RESORT, Santa Barbara, California

continental u.s. & canada

TOP HOTELS

➤ RESORTS (40 ROOMS OR MORE)

1. **SAN YSIDRO RANCH, A ROSEWOOD RESORT** Santa Barbara, California 96.17
2. **FOUR SEASONS RESORT JACKSON HOLE** Wyoming 93.43
2. **INN AT PALMETTO BLUFF** Bluffton, South Carolina 93.43
4. **WICKANINNISH INN** Tofino, British Columbia 93.14
5. **POST HOTEL & SPA** Lake Louise, Alberta 93.07
6. **SONNENALP RESORT OF VAIL** Colorado 92.52
7. **MONTAGE LAGUNA BEACH** California 92.15
8. **LITTLE NELL** Aspen, Colorado 91.78
9. **MEADOWOOD NAPA VALLEY** St. Helena, California 91.67
10. **AUBERGE DU SOLEIL** Rutherford, California 91.61
11. **HOUSTONIAN HOTEL, CLUB & SPA** Houston 91.51 ○
12. **BLACKBERRY FARM** Walland, Tennessee 91.46
13. **INTERCONTINENTAL MONTELUCIA RESORT & SPA** Paradise Valley, Arizona 91.45 ○
14. **WHITEFACE LODGE** Lake Placid, New York 91.25
15. **INN AT SPANISH BAY** Pebble Beach, California 91.20
16. **LODGE AT SEA ISLAND GOLF CLUB** Georgia 91.00
17. **THE SANCTUARY AT KIAWAH ISLAND GOLF RESORT** South Carolina 90.98
18. **HOTEL HEALDSBURG** Sonoma County, California 90.89
19. **STEIN ERIKSEN LODGE** Park City, Utah 90.88
20. **INN ON BILTMORE ESTATE** Asheville, North Carolina 90.76
21. **THE CLOISTER AT SEA ISLAND** Georgia 90.55
22. **PELICAN HILL RESORT** Newport Coast, California 90.49 ○
23. **CALISTOGA RANCH** Napa Valley, California 90.13
24. **RITZ-CARLTON** Naples, Florida 90.10
25. **BRAZILIAN COURT HOTEL & BEACH CLUB** Palm Beach, Florida 90.00
26. **THE BREAKERS** Palm Beach, Florida 89.95
27. **LODGE AT PEBBLE BEACH** California 89.86
28. **RITZ-CARLTON, LAGUNA NIGUEL** Dana Point, California 89.85
29. **L'AUBERGE DE SEDONA** Arizona 89.73
30. **MIRROR LAKE INN RESORT & SPA** Lake Placid, New York 89.71
31. **GRAND HOTEL MARRIOTT RESORT, GOLF CLUB & SPA** Point Clear, Alabama 89.62 ⑤ ○
31. **PONTE VEDRA INN & CLUB** Ponte Vedra Beach, Florida 89.62 ⑤
33. **ROYAL PALMS RESORT & SPA** Phoenix 89.58
34. **RITZ-CARLTON, BACHELOR GULCH** Beaver Creek, Colorado 89.58
35. **THE BROADMOOR** Colorado Springs 89.57
36. **FOUR SEASONS RESORT** Whistler, British Columbia 89.57
37. **RITZ-CARLTON** Amelia Island, Florida 89.52
38. **THE PHOENICIAN, A LUXURY COLLECTION RESORT** Scottsdale, Arizona 89.51
39. **RITZ-CARLTON GOLF RESORT** Naples, Florida 89.46
40. **SANDPEARL RESORT** Clearwater, Florida 89.30 ○
41. **STEPHANIE INN** Cannon Beach, Oregon 89.12
42. **VILLAGIO INN & SPA** Yountville, California 89.00 ○
43. **L'AUBERGE DEL MAR** Del Mar, California 88.86 ○
44. **PARK HYATT AVIARA RESORT (FORMERLY FOUR SEASONS RESORT, AVIARA)** Carlsbad, California 88.85
45. **ATLANTIC RESORT & SPA** Fort Lauderdale, Florida 88.73 ○
46. **RITZ-CARLTON** Half Moon Bay, California 88.72
47. **DISNEY'S GRAND FLORIDIAN RESORT & SPA** Orlando 88.64
48. **FOUR SEASONS RESORT THE BILTMORE** Santa Barbara, California 88.53
49. **WATERCOLOR INN & RESORT** Santa Rosa Beach, Florida 88.50
50. **THE GREENBRIER** White Sulphur Springs, West Virginia 88.48 ⑤

N⁰19 CONTINENTAL U.S. + CANADA RESORT
STEIN ERIKSEN LODGE, Park City, Utah

continental u.s. & canada

➤ LARGE CITY HOTELS (100 ROOMS OR MORE)
1. **TRUMP INTERNATIONAL HOTEL & TOWER** Chicago 94.32 ⊙
2. **THE PENINSULA** Chicago 93.09
3. **ROSEWOOD MANSION ON TURTLE CREEK** Dallas 92.28
4. **SUTTON PLACE HOTEL** Chicago 92.27 Ⓢ ⊙
5. **RITZ-CARLTON NEW YORK, CENTRAL PARK** 92.17
6. **THE PENINSULA** Beverly Hills 91.92
7. **FOUR SEASONS HOTEL** Chicago 91.77
8. **SOFITEL WASHINGTON D.C. LAFAYETTE SQUARE** 91.72
9. **THE ADOLPHUS** Dallas 91.48 Ⓢ ⊙
10. **ST. REGIS** New York City 90.97
11. **HERMITAGE HOTEL** Nashville 90.91 Ⓢ
12. **CHARLESTON PLACE** Charleston, South Carolina 90.68 Ⓢ
13. **HOTEL COMMONWEALTH** Boston 90.59 ⊙
14. **FOUR SEASONS HOTEL** Austin, Texas 90.55
15. **TOWNSEND HOTEL** Birmingham, Michigan 90.26 Ⓢ

16. **THE PENINSULA** New York City 90.05
17. **RITZ-CARLTON** San Francisco 89.98
18. **THE PALAZZO** Las Vegas 89.94
19. **FOUR SEASONS HOTEL** St. Louis 89.83 Ⓢ ⊙
20. **WYNN LAS VEGAS** 89.68 Ⓢ
21. **THE PLAZA** New York City 89.60
22. **TRUMP INTERNATIONAL HOTEL & TOWER** New York City 89.58
23. **ROSEWOOD CRESCENT HOTEL** Dallas 89.48
24. **FOUR SEASONS HOTEL** New York City 89.36
25. **THE NINES, A LUXURY COLLECTION HOTEL** Portland, Oregon 89.29 Ⓢ ⊙
26. **FOUR SEASONS HOTEL** San Francisco 89.15
27. **RITZ-CARLTON (A FOUR SEASONS HOTEL)** Chicago 89.12
28. **RITZ-CARLTON** Sarasota, Florida 88.94
29. **RITZ-CARLTON, TYSONS CORNER** McLean, Virginia 88.93
30. **HOTEL ZAZA** Dallas 88.90 ⊙
31. **BELLAGIO HOTEL & CASINO** Las Vegas 88.89 Ⓢ
32. **WINDSOR COURT HOTEL** New Orleans 88.84 Ⓢ
33. **FOUR SEASONS HOTEL** Boston 88.83
34. **RAPHAEL HOTEL** Kansas City, Missouri 88.80 Ⓢ
34. **UMSTEAD HOTEL & SPA** Cary, North Carolina 88.80 ⊙
36. **FOUR SEASONS HOTEL** Las Vegas 88.64 Ⓢ
37. **RITZ-CARLTON** Cleveland 88.53 Ⓢ
38. **HUNTINGTON HOTEL & NOB HILL SPA** San Francisco 88.52
38. **RITZ-CARLTON, PENTAGON CITY** Arlington, Virginia 88.52
40. **ENCORE WYNN LAS VEGAS** 88.52 Ⓢ ⊙
41. **MANDARIN ORIENTAL** San Francisco 88.47
42. **FOUR SEASONS HOTEL** Washington, D.C. 88.44
43. **SOFITEL CHICAGO WATER TOWER** 88.38 ⊙
44. **FOUR SEASONS HOTEL** Philadelphia 88.37
45. **MANDARIN ORIENTAL** New York City 88.26
46. **FOUR SEASONS HOTEL** Seattle 88.24
47. **ST. REGIS** San Francisco 88.22
48. **MANSION ON FORSYTH PARK** Savannah, Georgia 88.16 Ⓢ ⊙
49. **ST. REGIS** Washington, D.C. 88.15
50. **TAJ BOSTON** (formerly Ritz-Carlton) 88.00 Ⓢ ⊙

➤ SMALL CITY HOTELS (FEWER THAN 100 ROOMS)
1. **HOTEL BEL-AIR** (reopening in 2011) Los Angeles 93.67
2. **RITTENHOUSE HOTEL** Philadelphia 92.97
3. **AUBERGE SAINT-ANTOINE** Quebec City 92.80
4. **ELIOT HOTEL** Boston 90.15
4. **ROSEWOOD INN OF THE ANASAZI** Santa Fe, New Mexico 90.15
6. **PLANTERS INN** Charleston, South Carolina 89.70
7. **21C MUSEUM HOTEL** Louisville, Kentucky 89.60 Ⓢ ⊙
8. **THE JEFFERSON** Washington, D.C. 87.77 ⊙
9. **XV BEACON** Boston 87.71
10. **RITZ-CARLTON GEORGETOWN** Washington, D.C. 87.33

➤ INNS (FEWER THAN 40 ROOMS)
1. **TRIPLE CREEK RANCH** Darby, Montana 96.76
2. **WOODLANDS RESORT & INN** Summerville, South Carolina 94.12
3. **POST RANCH INN** Big Sur, California 93.13
4. **LITTLE PALM ISLAND RESORT & SPA** Little Torch Key, Florida 92.97
5. **FEARRINGTON HOUSE COUNTRY INN** Pittsboro, North Carolina 92.47

N°5 CONTINENTAL U.S. + CANADA LARGE CITY HOTEL
RITZ-CARLTON NEW YORK, CENTRAL PARK

N°1 CONTINENTAL U.S. + CANADA LARGE CITY HOTEL
TRUMP INTERNATIONAL HOTEL & TOWER, Chicago

TOP 25 U.S. HOTEL SPAS

1. **INN AT PALMETTO BLUFF** Bluffton, South Carolina 95.33
2. **MONTAGE LAGUNA BEACH** California 94.46
3. **MOHONK MOUNTAIN HOUSE** New Paltz, New York 94.06
4. **LA COSTA RESORT & SPA** Carlsbad, California 94.00
5. **DISNEY'S GRAND FLORIDIAN RESORT & SPA** Orlando 93.67
6. **HOUSTONIAN HOTEL, CLUB & SPA** Houston 93.13 ⊖
7. **GROVE PARK INN RESORT & SPA** Asheville, North Carolina 93.02
8. **POST RANCH INN** Big Sur, California 92.81
9. **INN AT SPANISH BAY** Pebble Beach, California 91.84
10. **FAIRMONT SCOTTSDALE PRINCESS** Arizona 91.33
11. **BORGATA HOTEL CASINO & SPA** Atlantic City, New Jersey 91.25
11. **WYNN LAS VEGAS** 91.25
13. **JW MARRIOTT CAMELBACK INN RESORT & SPA** Scottsdale, Arizona 91.23

14. **MANDARIN ORIENTAL** Miami 91.14
15. **CALISTOGA RANCH** Napa Valley, California 90.88
16. **SANCTUARY AT KIAWAH ISLAND GOLF RESORT** South Carolina 90.36
17. **THE PHOENICIAN, A LUXURY COLLECTION RESORT** Scottsdale, Arizona 90.12
18. **PARK HYATT AVIARA RESORT** (formerly Four Seasons Resort Aviara) Carlsbad, California 89.81
19. **RITZ-CARLTON HALF MOON BAY** California 89.69
20. **RITZ-CARLTON AMELIA ISLAND** Florida 89.60
21. **HAWKS CAY RESORT & MARINA** Duck Key, Florida 89.58 ⊖
22. **ST. REGIS MONARCH BEACH** Dana Point, California 89.50
23. **MONTEREY PLAZA HOTEL & SPA** California 89.38
23. **THE PENINSULA** Chicago 89.38
25. **HOTEL HERSHEY** Pennsylvania 89.22 ⊖

N⁰1 CONTINENTAL U.S. + CANADA HOTEL SPA
INN AT PALMETTO BLUFF, Bluffton, South Carolina

TOP 25 HOTELS

➤ RESORTS

1. **FOUR SEASONS RESORT HUALALAI** Hawaii 92.74
2. **HALEKULANI** Oahu 92.43
3. **KAHALA HOTEL & RESORT** Oahu 91.53
4. **FOUR SEASONS RESORT LANAI, THE LODGE AT KOELE** 91.39
5. **FOUR SEASONS RESORT MAUI AT WAILEA** 89.91
6. **FOUR SEASONS RESORT LANAI AT MANELE BAY** 89.52
7. **MAUNA LANI BAY HOTEL & BUNGALOWS** Hawaii 88.96
8. **HOTEL HANA-MAUI & HONUA SPA** 88.64
9. **GRAND HYATT KAUAI RESORT & SPA** 88.41
10. **FAIRMONT KEA LANI** Maui 87.69
11. **RITZ-CARLTON KAPALUA** Maui 87.49
12. **MAUNA KEA BEACH HOTEL** Hawaii 87.47
13. **ROYAL HAWAIIAN, A LUXURY COLLECTION RESORT** Oahu 87.41
14. **HYATT REGENCY MAUI RESORT & SPA** 87.20
15. **MAKENA BEACH & GOLF RESORT** Maui 86.67
16. **ST. REGIS PRINCEVILLE RESORT** Kauai 85.95
17. **HYATT REGENCY WAIKIKI BEACH RESORT & SPA** Oahu 85.52
18. **JW MARRIOTT IHILANI RESORT & SPA** Oahu 85.17
19. **KONA VILLAGE RESORT** Hawaii 84.82
20. **EMBASSY SUITES WAIKIKI BEACH WALK** Oahu 84.59 $ ✪
21. **OUTRIGGER WAIKIKI ON THE BEACH** Oahu 84.18 $
22. **TURTLE BAY RESORT** Oahu 83.72
23. **WAILEA BEACH MARRIOTT RESORT & SPA** Maui 83.69
24. **GRAND WAILEA** Maui 83.47
25. **KAUAI MARRIOTT RESORT & BEACH CLUB** 83.31

hawaii

TOP 5 HOTEL SPAS

1. **FOUR SEASONS RESORT HUALALAI** Hawaii 93.42
2. **GRAND WAILEA** Maui 90.92 $
3. **FOUR SEASONS RESORT MAUI AT WAILEA** 89.29
4. **FAIRMONT ORCHID** Hawaii 89.06
5. **RITZ-CARLTON KAPALUA** Maui 89.05

N°1 HAWAII HOTEL SPA + RESORT
FOUR SEASONS RESORT HUALALAI

Nº2 CARIBBEAN HOTEL
JADE MOUNTAIN, St. Lucia

the caribbean, bermuda & the bahamas

TOP 25 HOTELS

1. **NISBET PLANTATION BEACH CLUB** Nevis 95.75
2. **JADE MOUNTAIN** St. Lucia 94.91
3. **JAMAICA INN & SPA** Ocho Rios, Jamaica 93.50
4. **COUPLES TOWER ISLE** St. Mary, Jamaica 92.47
5. **COUPLES SWEPT AWAY** Negril, Jamaica 91.38
6. **COUPLES SANS SOUCI** Ocho Rios, Jamaica 91.00
7. **TUCKER'S POINT HOTEL & SPA** Bermuda 90.59 ✪
8. **SANDY LANE** Barbados 90.24
9. **PETER ISLAND RESORT & SPA** British Virgin Islands 89.85
10. **RITZ-CARLTON** Grand Cayman, Cayman Islands 89.50
11. **CURTAIN BLUFF RESORT** Antigua 89.33
12. **REGENT PALMS** Turks and Caicos 89.19 ✪
13. **HÔTEL LE TOINY** St. Bart's 89.18
14. **ONE&ONLY OCEAN CLUB** Paradise Island, Bahamas 89.14
15. **REEFS HOTEL & CLUB** Bermuda 89.08
16. **HÔTEL GUANAHANI & SPA** St. Bart's 88.71
17. **HOTEL SAINT-BARTH ISLE DE FRANCE** St. Bart's 88.60
18. **SANDALS WHITEHOUSE EUROPEAN VILLAGE & SPA** Jamaica 88.50
19. **COUPLES NEGRIL** Jamaica 88.41
20. **ANSE CHASTANET RESORT** St. Lucia 88.00
20. **LADERA** St. Lucia 88.00
22. **EDEN ROCK** St. Bart's 87.57
23. **PARROT CAY** Turks and Caicos 87.40
24. **SANDALS REGENCY LA TOC ST. LUCIA GOLF RESORT & SPA** 87.33 ✪
24. **ROUND HILL HOTEL & VILLAS** Montego Bay, Jamaica 87.33

TOP 10 HOTEL SPAS

1. **COUPLES TOWER ISLE** St. Mary, Jamaica 96.00 ⑤
2. **COUPLES SANS SOUCI** Ocho Rios, Jamaica 93.36 ⑤
3. **COUPLES SWEPT AWAY** Negril, Jamaica 92.28 ⑤
4. **ONE&ONLY OCEAN CLUB** Paradise Island, Bahamas 90.24
5. **PETER ISLAND RESORT** British Virgin Islands 89.62
6. **ROSEWOOD LITTLE DIX BAY** Virgin Gorda, British Virgin Islands 89.23
7. **COVE ATLANTIS** Paradise Island, Bahamas 87.68
8. **FAIRMONT SOUTHAMPTON** Bermuda 87.50
9. **HALF MOON** Montego Bay, Jamaica 87.22
9. **LA SAMANNA** St. Martin 87.22

Nº1 CARIBBEAN HOTEL
NISBET PLANTATION BEACH CLUB, Nevis

mexico

TOP 5 HOTEL SPAS

1. **ESPERANZA, AN AUBERGE RESORT** Los Cabos 93.50
2. **CASAMAGNA MARRIOTT PUERTO VALLARTA RESORT & SPA** 92.78
3. **LE MÉRIDIEN CANCÚN RESORT & SPA** 92.22
4. **FOUR SEASONS RESORT** Punta Mita 86.54
5. **PUEBLO BONITO SUNSET BEACH RESORT & SPA** Los Cabos 85.77

TOP HOTELS

➤ RESORTS

1. **ESPERANZA, AN AUBERGE RESORT** Los Cabos 92.91
2. **ONE&ONLY PALMILLA** Los Cabos 92.69
3. **FOUR SEASONS RESORT** Punta Mita 90.92
4. **LAS VENTANAS AL PARAÍSO, A ROSEWOOD RESORT** Los Cabos 90.40
5. **RITZ-CARLTON** Cancún 89.84
6. **PUEBLO BONITO PACIFICA RESORT & SPA** Los Cabos 89.52 ❋
7. **LAS BRISAS** Acapulco 89.28
8. **CASAMAGNA MARRIOTT CANCÚN RESORT** 87.83 $
9. **LE MÉRIDIEN CANCÚN RESORT & SPA** 87.56
10. **MELIÁ CABO REAL ALL-INCLUSIVE BEACH & GOLF RESORT** Los Cabos 87.29 $ ❋
11. **FAIRMONT MAYAKOBA** Riviera Maya 87.20 $
11. **FIESTA AMERICANA GRAND CORAL BEACH CANCÚN RESORT & SPA** 87.20 $
13. **HILTON CANCÚN GOLF & SPA RESORT** 87.04 $ ❋
14. **JW MARRIOTT CANCÚN RESORT & SPA** 86.00 $
15. **PUEBLO BONITO SUNSET BEACH RESORT & SPA** Los Cabos 84.95
16. **DREAMS CANCÚN RESORT & SPA** (formerly Camino Real) 84.53 ❋
16. **TIDES ZIHUATANEJO** 84.53
18. **FAIRMONT ACAPULCO PRINCESS** 84.36
19. **GRAN MELIÁ CANCÚN** 83.60 $ ❋
20. **BARCELÓ MAYA BEACH** Riviera Maya 82.44 $ ❋

➤ CITY HOTELS

1. **FOUR SEASONS HOTEL MÉXICO, D.F.** Mexico City 95.00
2. **JW MARRIOTT HOTEL MEXICO CITY** 89.14
3. **PRESIDENTE INTERCONTINENTAL** Mexico City 82.00

N°1 MEXICO RESORT + HOTEL SPA
ESPERANZA, AN AUBERGE RESORT, Los Cabos

central & south america

TOP 5 HOTEL SPAS

1. **FOUR SEASONS RESORT** Carmelo, Uruguay 92.22
2. **LLAO LLAO HOTEL & RESORT, GOLF-SPA** Bariloche, Argentina 91.36
3. **FOUR SEASONS HOTEL** Buenos Aires 90.26
4. **FOUR SEASONS RESORT COSTA RICA AT PENINSULA PAPAGAYO** 89.58
5. **TABACÓN GRAND SPA THERMAL RESORT** Arenal, Costa Rica 87.08

TOP HOTELS

➤ RESORTS

1. **BLANCANEAUX LODGE** San Ignacio, Belize 92.73
2. **FOUR SEASONS RESORT** Carmelo, Uruguay 91.53
3. **INKATERRA MACHU PICCHU PUEBLO HOTEL** Peru 90.69
4. **FOUR SEASONS RESORT COSTA RICA AT PENINSULA PAPAGAYO** 88.44
5. **MACHU PICCHU SANCTUARY LODGE** Peru 88.21
6. **LLAO LLAO HOTEL & RESORT, GOLF-SPA** Bariloche, Argentina 87.68
7. **TURTLE INN** Placencia, Belize 86.29
8. **TABACÓN GRAND SPA THERMAL RESORT** Arenal, Costa Rica 83.12 ✱
9. **LOS SUEÑOS MARRIOTT OCEAN & GOLF RESORT** Playa Herradura, Costa Rica 82.53 $
10. **JW MARRIOTT GUANACASTE RESORT & SPA** Guanacaste, Costa Rica 81.33 $ ✱

➤ CITY HOTELS

1. **ALVEAR PALACE HOTEL** Buenos Aires 92.25
2. **PALACIO DUHAU-PARK HYATT** Buenos Aires 92.00
3. **RITZ-CARLTON** Santiago, Chile 91.65
4. **FOUR SEASONS HOTEL** Buenos Aires 91.00
5. **HOTEL MONASTERIO** Cuzco, Peru 90.88
6. **HOTEL CASA SANTO DOMINGO** Antigua, Guatemala 90.00 $
7. **JW MARRIOTT HOTEL** Lima, Peru 89.09
8. **JW MARRIOTT HOTEL** Quito, Ecuador 88.35 $ ✱
9. **SOFITEL BUENOS AIRES** 87.81 ✱
10. **HILTON BUENOS AIRES** 86.44 ✱

N°4 CENTRAL + SOUTH AMERICA SPA
FOUR SEASONS RESORT COSTA RICA AT PENINSULA PAPAGAYO

europe

TOP HOTELS

➤ LARGE CITY HOTELS
1. **OLISSIPPO LAPA PALACE** Lisbon 94.60
2. **HÔTEL DE CRILLON** Paris 94.40
3. **FOUR SEASONS HOTEL** Dublin 93.68 🟢
4. **STAFFORD LONDON** 93.44
5. **FOUR SEASONS HOTEL GRESHAM PALACE** Budapest 92.96
6. **FOUR SEASONS HÔTEL GEORGE V** Paris 92.76
7. **FOUR SEASONS HOTEL** Milan 91.77
8. **HOTEL IMPERIAL, A LUXURY COLLECTION HOTEL** Vienna 91.52
9. **PARK HYATT PARIS-VENDÔME** 91.33
10. **FOUR SEASONS HOTEL FIRENZE** Florence 91.27
11. **HÔTEL DE PARIS MONTE-CARLO** Monaco 90.91
12. **THE MERRION** Dublin 90.67
13. **HOTEL DE RUSSIE** Rome 90.59 ✪
14. **BROWN'S HOTEL** London 90.43 ✪
15. **FOUR SEASONS HOTEL** Prague 90.33

➤ SMALL CITY HOTELS
1. **THE LANESBOROUGH, A ST. REGIS HOTEL** London 93.47
2. **MANDARIN ORIENTAL** Prague 92.94 ✪
3. **FOUR SEASONS HOTEL ISTANBUL AT SULTANAHMET** 92.63
4. **BAUR AU LAC** Zurich 92.20
5. **THE GORING** London 91.06
6. **HOTEL HASSLER ROMA** Rome 90.94
7. **ROYAL CRESCENT HOTEL** Bath, England 90.90
8. **HOTEL GRITTI PALACE, A LUXURY COLLECTION HOTEL** Venice 89.94
9. **THE MILESTONE** London 89.47
10. **HOTEL GOLDENER HIRSCH, A LUXURY COLLECTION HOTEL**
    Salzburg, Austria 88.08

➤ RESORTS
1. **PALAZZO SASSO** Ravello, Italy 95.17
2. **LE SIRENUSE** Positano, Italy 94.88
3. **VILLA D'ESTE** Cernobbio, Italy 93.66
4. **HOTEL SPLENDIDO** Portofino, Italy 93.52
5. **HOTEL VILLA SAN MICHELE** Fiesole, Italy 91.80
6. **SHEEN FALLS LODGE** County Kerry, Ireland 91.47
7. **HOTEL SANTA CATERINA** Amalfi Coast, Italy 90.72
8. **IL SAN PIETRO** Positano, Italy 90.71
9. **ASHFORD CASTLE** County Mayo, Ireland 90.63
10. **DROMOLAND CASTLE** County Clare, Ireland 90.62

➤ INNS AND SMALL COUNTRY HOTELS
1. **DOMAINE DES HAUTS DE LOIRE** Onzain, France 95.00 🟢
2. **HÔTEL CHÂTEAU EZA** Èze Village, France 93.33
3. **CHÂTEAU DE LA CHÈVRE D'OR** Èze Village, France 92.71
4. **LA COLOMBE D'OR HÔTEL** St.-Paul-de-Vence, France 91.67
5. **LES CRAYÈRES** Reims, France 91.09
6. **HOTEL VILLA CIPRIANI** Asolo, Italy 90.11
7. **KATIKIES HOTEL** Santorini, Greece 89.33
8. **L'OUSTAU DE BAUMANIÈRE** Les Baux-de-Provence, France 89.14
9. **IL FALCONIERE** Cortona, Italy 88.75
10. **VILLA GALLICI** Aix-en-Provence, France 87.05

N°2 EUROPE SMALL CITY HOTEL
MANDARIN ORIENTAL, Prague

africa & the middle east

TOP HOTELS

➤ LODGES AND RESORTS

1. **FAIRMONT MARA SAFARI CLUB** Masai Mara, Kenya 96.31
2. **ROYAL MALEWANE** Kruger National Park, South Africa 94.67
3. **SINGITA SABI SAND (EBONY LODGE, BOULDERS LODGE, CASTLETON CAMP)** Sabi Sand Reserve, South Africa 94.67
4. **SINGITA KRUGER NATIONAL PARK (LEBOMBO LODGE, SWENI LODGE)** South Africa 94.25
5. **LONDOLOZI PRIVATE GAME RESERVE** Sabi Sand Reserve, South Africa 94.18
6. **TORTILIS CAMP AMBOSELI,** Kenya 94.12
7. **&BEYOND KICHWA TEMBO MASAI MARA TENTED CAMP** Kenya 93.71
8. **TWELVE APOSTLES HOTEL & SPA** Cape Town 93.62
9. **MALAMALA GAME RESERVE** South Africa 93.07
10. **ROYAL LIVINGSTONE** Victoria Falls, Zambia 92.59
11. **SERENGETI SOPA LODGE** Tanzania 92.57
12. **FAIRMONT MOUNT KENYA SAFARI CLUB** Nanyuki, Kenya 92.29
13. **SANCTUARY CHIEF'S CAMP** Okavango Delta, Botswana 90.40
14. **NGORONGORO CRATER LODGE** Tanzania 89.90
15. **NGORONGORO SOPA LODGE** Tanzania 88.55
16. **ZANZIBAR SERENA INN** Tanzania 86.13 ✪
17. **NGORONGORO SERENA SAFARI LODGE** Tanzania 83.82
18. **SERENGETI SERENA SAFARI LODGE** Tanzania 83.78
19. **AMBOSELI SERENA SAFARI LODGE** Amboseli Game Reserve, Kenya 82.80
20. **LAKE MANYARA SERENA SAFARI LODGE** Tanzania 82.09

➤ CITY HOTELS

1. **FOUR SEASONS HOTEL CAIRO AT THE FIRST RESIDENCE** 93.27
2. **CAPE GRACE** Cape Town 92.52
3. **BURJ AL ARAB** Dubai 91.57 ✪
4. **SAXON BOUTIQUE HOTEL, VILLAS & SPA** Johannesburg 90.86
5. **FOUR SEASONS HOTEL ALEXANDRIA AT SAN STEFANO** Egypt 90.25
6. **FOUR SEASONS HOTEL AT NILE PLAZA** Cairo 89.95
7. **THE WESTCLIFF** Johannesburg 89.22
8. **MOUNT NELSON HOTEL** Cape Town 87.64
9. **TABLE BAY HOTEL** Cape Town 87.17
10. **MICHELANGELO HOTEL** Johannesburg 87.11
11. **KING DAVID HOTEL** Jerusalem 87.02
12. **MENA HOUSE OBEROI** Cairo 86.87 ⑤
13. **FAIRMONT THE NORFOLK HOTEL** Nairobi, Kenya 86.76
14. **LA MAMOUNIA** Marrakesh, Morocco 86.74
15. **FOUR SEASONS HOTEL** Amman, Jordan 86.72

N°2 AFRICA + THE MIDDLE EAST CITY HOTEL
CAPE GRACE, Cape Town, South Africa

N°1 ASIA RESORT
OBEROI VANYAVILAS, Ranthambore, India

asia

TOP HOTELS

➤ RESORTS
1. **OBEROI VANYAVILAS** Ranthambore, India 97.26
2. **OBEROI AMARVILAS** Agra, India 95.94
3. **OBEROI RAJVILAS** Jaipur, India 94.78
4. **OBEROI UDAIVILAS** Udaipur, India 94.71
5. **FOUR SEASONS RESORT** Chiang Mai, Thailand 93.95
6. **HÔTEL DE LA PAIX** Siem Reap, Cambodia 93.75 ☉
7. **RAMBAGH PALACE** Jaipur, India 93.60
8. **TAJ LAKE PALACE** Udaipur, India 93.46
9. **MANDARIN ORIENTAL DHARA DHEVI** Chiang Mai, Thailand 93.26
10. **UMAID BHAWAN PALACE** Jodhpur, India 90.96 ☉
11. **FOUR SEASONS RESORT BALI AT JIMBARAN BAY** 90.80
12. **ANANTARA GOLDEN TRIANGLE RESORT & SPA** Chiang Rai, Thailand 90.67
13. **AMANPURI** Phuket, Thailand 90.60
14. **DISCOVERY SHORES** Boracay, Philippines 90.35 ☉
15. **JW MARRIOTT PHUKET RESORT & SPA** Thailand 89.03

➤ CITY HOTELS
1. **THE PENINSULA** Bangkok 95.69
2. **FOUR SEASONS HOTEL** Singapore 94.75
3. **SHANGRI-LA HOTEL** Singapore 94.32
4. **THE PENINSULA** Hong Kong 94.11
5. **TAJ MAHAL PALACE** Mumbai 93.83
6. **RITZ-CARLTON BEIJING, FINANCIAL STREET** 93.04
7. **MANDARIN ORIENTAL** Bangkok 92.89
8. **THE PENINSULA** Beijing 92.88
9. **MANDARIN ORIENTAL** Hong Kong 92.84
10. **LEELA PALACE KEMPINSKI** Bengaluru (Bangalore), India 92.27 ☉
11. **FOUR SEASONS HOTEL** Hong Kong 91.86
12. **ISLAND SHANGRI-LA** Hong Kong 91.43
13. **MAKATI SHANGRI-LA** Manila 91.03
14. **SOFITEL LEGEND METROPOLE** Hanoi, Vietnam 90.87 ⑤
15. **THE PENINSULA** Manila 90.82 ☉
16. **RAFFLES HOTEL** Singapore 90.76
17. **FOUR SEASONS HOTEL** Bangkok 90.72
18. **ST. REGIS** Beijing 90.67
19. **FULLERTON HOTEL** Singapore 90.50
20. **THE IMPERIAL** New Delhi 90.27
21. **ST. REGIS** Shanghai 89.91
22. **PUDONG SHANGRI-LA** Shanghai 89.90
22. **FOUR SEASONS HOTEL** Shanghai 89.90
24. **MANDARIN ORIENTAL** Kuala Lumpur, Malaysia 89.69
25. **LE MÉRIDIEN** Bangkok 89.60

TOP 10 HOTEL SPAS

1. **FOUR SEASONS RESORT BALI AT JIMBARAN BAY** 96.07 ⑤
2. **FOUR SEASONS RESORT** Chiang Mai, Thailand 95.00
2. **MANDARIN ORIENTAL** Hong Kong 95.00
4. **FOUR SEASONS HOTEL** Shanghai 94.09 ⑤
5. **MANDARIN ORIENTAL** Bangkok 93.85 ⑤
6. **JW MARRIOTT PHUKET RESORT & SPA** Thailand 92.92 ⑤
7. **ANANTARA GOLDEN TRIANGLE RESORT & SPA** Chiang Rai, Thailand 91.00 ⑤
8. **RAFFLES GRAND HOTEL D'ANGKOR** Siem Reap, Cambodia 90.00 ⑤
9. **SHANGRI-LA'S MACTAN RESORT & SPA** Cebu, Philippines 87.50 ⑤
10. **INTERCONTINENTAL** Hong Kong 86.67 ⑤

Nº4 ASIA CITY HOTEL
THE PENINSULA, Hong Kong

N° 1 AUSTRALIA + NEW ZEALAND + THE SOUTH PACIFIC LODGES AND RESORTS
HUKA LODGE, Taupo, New Zealand

australia, new zealand & the south pacific

TOP HOTELS

➤ **LODGES AND RESORTS**
1. **HUKA LODGE** Taupo, New Zealand 91.25
2. **HAYMAN GREAT BARRIER REEF** Australia 90.00
3. **INTERCONTINENTAL BORA BORA RESORT & THALASSO SPA** French Polynesia 89.87
4. **VOYAGES LONGITUDE 131°** Ayers Rock, Australia 84.19
5. **INTERCONTINENTAL RESORT & SPA** Moorea, French Polynesia 81.17

➤ **CITY HOTELS**
1. **THE LANGHAM** Melbourne 91.50 Ⓢ
2. **THE GEORGE** Christchurch, New Zealand 88.13
3. **PARK HYATT** Sydney 87.68
4. **PARK HYATT** Melbourne 87.06
5. **SHANGRI-LA HOTEL** Sydney 86.89 Ⓢ
6. **HILTON** Auckland 86.71
7. **PULLMAN (FORMERLY HYATT REGENCY)** Auckland 86.20 Ⓢ
8. **STAMFORD PLAZA** Auckland 85.60 Ⓢ
9. **SYDNEY HARBOUR MARRIOTT HOTEL AT CIRCULAR QUAY** 85.30 Ⓢ
10. **INTERCONTINENTAL** Sydney 84.88 Ⓢ

Nº5 AUSTRALIA + NEW ZEALAND + THE SOUTH PACIFIC CITY HOTEL
SHANGRI-LA HOTEL, Sydney, Australia

Sierra Mar restaurant at Post
Ranch Inn, in Big Sur, California.

T+L 500

NITED STATES CANADA ANGUILLA ANTIGUA BAHAMAS BARBADOS BERM
RITISH VIRGIN ISLANDS CAYMAN ISLANDS JAMAICA NEVIS ST. BART'S ST. L
URKS & CAICOS ARGENTINA BELIZE CHILE COSTA RICA ECUADOR GUATEM
EXICO PERU URUGUAY AUSTRIA BELGIUM CZECH REPUBLIC ENGLAND FR
ERMANY HUNGARY IRELAND ITALY MONACO NETHERLANDS POLAND PC
OTLAND SPAIN SWEDEN SWITZERLAND TURKEY BOTSWANA EGYPT ISRA
NYA MOROCCO SOUTH AFRICA UNITED ARAB EMIRATES ZAMBIA CAMBC

United States

ALABAMA

POINT CLEAR

Grand Hotel Marriott Resort, Golf Club & Spa (89.62) A 405-room resort on 550 acres; the new pool, tennis, and fitness center fronts a private lake. 800/228-9290 or 251/928-9201; marriottgrand.com; doubles from $.

ALASKA

GIRDWOOD

Hotel Alyeska (86.93) In the valley of a ski mountain 40 miles south of Anchorage, a 301-room hotel; coming in 2012, a revamped high-speed lift. 800/880-3880 or 907/754-2111; alyeskaresort.com; doubles from $$.

ARIZONA

CAREFREE

Boulders Resort & Golden Door Spa (86.59) Set in a 12-million-year-old rock outcropping, 221 casitas and villas, with a legendary spa. 866/397-6520 or 480/488-9009; theboulders.com; doubles from $.

PHOENIX/SCOTTSDALE

Four Seasons Resort Scottsdale at Troon North (86.72) A 210-room pueblo-inspired property with a bi-level pool and a telescope for stargazing. 10600 E. Crescent Moon Dr., Scottsdale; 800/332-3442 or 480/515-5700; fourseasons.com; doubles from $$.

InterContinental Montelucia Resort & Spa (91.45) Andalusian-style hotel with a lively poolside scene. 4949 E. Lincoln Dr., Scottsdale; 800/327-0200; icmontelucia.com; doubles from $$.

JW Marriott Camelback Inn Resort & Spa (86.78) Family-friendly resort, with 453 Pueblo-style casitas and 27 suites, plus a putting green. 5402 E. Lincoln Dr., Scottsdale; 800/228-9290 or

480/948-1700; camelbackinn.com; doubles from $$$.

The Phoenician, a Luxury Collection Resort (89.51) A classic resort on 250 acres, with new restaurants such as the Relish Burger Bistro. 6000 E. Camelback Rd., Scottsdale; 800/325-3589 or 480/941-8200; thephoenician.com; doubles from $$$$.

Royal Palms Resort & Spa (89.58) A Spanish colonial–style mansion on nine acres. 5200 E. Camelback Rd., Phoenix; 800/672-6011 or 602/840-3610; royalpalmshotel.com; doubles from $$.

SEDONA

Enchantment Resort & Mii amo Spa (88.08) In a red-rock canyon, 218 adobe rooms and casitas, plus the award-winning spa. 800/826-4180 or 928/282-2900; enchantmentresort.com; doubles from $$.

L'Auberge de Sedona (89.73) Romantic creekside retreat fresh from a $25 million expansion that added 31 cottages. 800/272-6777 or 928/282-1661; lauberge.com; doubles from $$.

TUCSON

Arizona Inn (87.09) A 95-room estate (original Audubon prints; lush gardens) that evokes a bygone era. 800/933-1093 or 520/325-1541; arizonainn.com; doubles from $$.

CALIFORNIA

BIG SUR

Post Ranch Inn (93.13) Forty-one solar-powered rooms in cottages overlooking the Pacific. 800/527-2200 or 831/667-2200; postranchinn.com; doubles from $$$, including breakfast.

Ventana Inn & Spa (87.08) Adults-only retreat of 55 rooms and three

villas fitted with wood-burning fireplaces. 800/628-6500 or 831/667-2331; ventanainn.com; doubles from $$$, including breakfast.

CARMEL

Bernardus Lodge (87.57) Fresh flowers and bottles from the winery next door are stocked in all 57 rooms at this Provençal-style hotel. 888/648-9463 or 831/658-3400; bernardus.com; doubles from $$$.

Hyatt Carmel Highlands (87.58) Craftsman-style hotel with redesigned rooms and floor-to-ceiling windows, most overlooking the coast. 800/233-1234 or 831/620-1234; hyatt.com; doubles from $$$.

L'Auberge Carmel (87.06) A 20-room inn around a brick courtyard; the restaurant is known for its 4,500-bottle wine cellar. 831/624-8578; laubergecarmel.com; doubles from $$$, including breakfast.

DEL MAR

L'Auberge Del Mar (88.86) One block from the beach, 120 light-filled rooms and a renovated spa. 800/245-9757 or 858/259-1515; laubergedelmar.com; doubles from $$.

HALF MOON BAY

Ritz-Carlton (88.72) Two golf courses and 261 rooms (some with patio fire pits). A butler is on hand to assist with s'mores. 800/241-3333 or 650/712-7000; ritzcarlton.com; doubles from $$.

LOS ANGELES AREA

Beverly Hills Hotel & Bungalows (87.77) The pink palace opened two new bungalows in March. 9641 Sunset Blvd., Beverly Hills; 800/283-8885 or 310/276-2251; beverlyhillshotel.com; doubles from $$$.

Beverly Wilshire, a Four Seasons Hotel (87.29) Reinvented 1928

legend at Rodeo Drive. There's a Rolls-Royce for guest transportation. 9500 Wilshire Blvd., Beverly Hills; 800/332-3442 or 310/275-5200; fourseasons.com; doubles from $$.

Fairmont Miramar Hotel & Bungalows (86.42) A seven-minute walk from the Pacific, bungalows and a 10-story tower, plus a spa, restaurant, and BMW cruiser bikes. 101 Wilshire Blvd., Santa Monica; 800/441-1414 or 310/576-7777; fairmont.com; doubles from $$.

Hotel Bel-Air (93.67) A Dorchester Collection retreat reopening this summer, with 103 rooms (including 12 new canyon-view suites), a spa, and a pond inhabited by swans. 701 Stone Canyon Rd., Los Angeles; 800/648-4097 or 310/472-1211; hotelbelair.com; doubles from $$$.

Montage Beverly Hills (87.71) Built in 2008 yet exudes old-world glamour in the rooms and piano bar. Smart tech amenities lure business travelers. 225 N. Canon Dr., Beverly Hills; 888/860-0788 or 310/860-7800; montagebeverlyhills.com; doubles from $$$.

Peninsula Beverly Hills (91.92) Modeled after a French estate, the 196-room oasis attracts high-wattage guests at the rooftop pool bar. 9882 S. Santa Monica Blvd., Beverly Hills; 866/382-8388 or 310/551-2888; peninsula.com; doubles from $$$.

NAPA/SONOMA

Auberge du Soleil (91.61) Here, 48 rooms and two vine-covered cottages, plus a French restaurant with stellar sunset views of wine country. Rutherford; 800/348-5406 or 707/963-1211; aubergedusoleil. com; doubles from $$$$.

Calistoga Ranch, an Auberge Resort *(90.13)* Set among canyon streams and oak trees, 48 rustic cabins, with open-air showers. Calistoga; 800/942-4220 or 707/254-2800; calistogaranch.com; doubles from $$$.

Carneros Inn *(86.38)* Eighty-six cozy cottages (soaking tubs; heated bathroom floors), plus three pools and a spa. Napa; 888/400-9000 or 707/299-4900; thecarnerosinn.com; doubles from $$$.

Hotel Healdsburg *(90.89)* Charlie Palmer's minimalist haven, with a celebrated restaurant. Healdsburg; 800/889-7188 or 707/431-2800; hotelhealdsburg.com; doubles from $$, including breakfast.

Meadowood Napa Valley *(91.67)* An estate where rooms sit among fir trees; activities include wine classes and croquet. St. Helena; 800/458-8080 or 707/963-3646; meadowood. com; doubles from $$$.

Villagio Inn & Spa *(89.00)* Many of the 112 rooms overlook a blue-tiled waterway at this Italianate hotel, close to the French Laundry. Yountville; 800/351-1133 or 707/944-8877; villagio.com; doubles from $$, including breakfast.

ORANGE COUNTY
Montage Laguna Beach *(92.15)* A 250-room Craftsman-style resort—now with a three-bedroom beach house for rent. Laguna Beach; 866/271-6951 or 949/715-6000; montagelaguna beach.com; doubles from $$$$.

Pelican Hill Resort *(90.49)* The 332 roomy bungalows recall seaside Tuscany. A must-see: the circular

coliseum pool. Newport Coast; 800/820-6800 or 949/467-6800; pelicanhill.com; doubles from $$$.

Ritz-Carlton, Laguna Niguel *(89.85)* Four-story hideaway with marine-oriented programs—from surf lessons to eco-excursions—above a legendary wave break. Dana Point; 800/241-3333; ritzcarlton.com; doubles from $$.

St. Regis Monarch Beach *(86.80)* White-glove butler service and 400 super-sleek rooms. There's also seaside golf and a private beach club. Dana Point; 877/787-3447 or 949/234-3200; stregis.com; doubles from $$$.

PASADENA
Langham Huntington *(86.67)* Dignified 1907 property (380 rooms, a spa, and a new French-inspired restaurant) at the base of the San Gabriel Mountains. 800/588-9141 or 626/568-3900; langhamhotels.com; doubles from $$.

PEBBLE BEACH
Inn at Spanish Bay *(91.20)* Low-lying hotel on the Monterey Peninsula. Guests have access to the Pebble Beach Golf Links. 800/654-9300 or 831/647-7500; pebblebeach. com; doubles from $$$.

Lodge at Pebble Beach *(89.86)* A 1919 Georgian-style golf haven, where many of the 161 rooms have wood-burning fireplaces. 800/654-9300 or 831/624-3811; pebblebeach. com; doubles from $$$.

SAN DIEGO AREA
Grand Del Mar *(87.36)* Family-friendly resort that exudes European refinement. 5300 Grand Del Mar Court, San Diego; 888/314-2030 or 858/314-2000; thegranddelmar.com; doubles from $$.

The front lounge area at California's Calistoga Ranch.

La Valencia Hotel *(87.09)* 1926 hideaway with murals and mosaics, in a tiny suburb. La Jolla; 800/451-0772 or 858/454-0771; lavalencia. com; doubles from $$.

Lodge at Torrey Pines *(86.36)* Craftsman-style golf resort on a cliff next to a 2,000-acre nature preserve. La Jolla; 800/656-0087 or 858/453-4420; lodgetorreypines. com; doubles from $$.

Park Hyatt Aviara Resort (formerly Four Seasons Resort Aviara) *(88.85)* Outdoor living rooms and an Arnold Palmer golf course in a seaside setting. Carlsbad; 877/875-4658 or 760/

448-1234; park.hyatt.com; doubles from $$.

Westgate Hotel *(87.65)* Opulent 223-room hotel filled with antiques and 18th-century tapestries. 1055 2nd Ave., San Diego; 800/522-1564 or 619/238-1818; westgatehotel.com; doubles from $$.

SAN FRANCISCO
Fairmont San Francisco *(86.78)* A 1907 palace with restored details, an organic garden, and a new media lounge. 950 Mason St.; 800/441-1414; fairmont.com; doubles from $.

Four Seasons Hotel *(89.15)* In the Yerba Buena Arts District, the city's

largest rooms, with notable furnishings such as Herman Miller Eames chairs. 757 Market St.; 800/332-3442 or 415/633-3000; fourseasons.com; doubles from $$.

Huntington Hotel & Nob Hill Spa (*88.52*) A 1924 hotel with town-house touches (plus tea at check-in). 1075 California St.; 800/227-4683 or 415/474-5400; huntingtonhotel.com; doubles from $$.

Mandarin Oriental (*88.47*) Occupying the top 11 floors of the city's third-tallest building, 158 rooms in warm reds and golds. 222 Sansome St.; 800/526-6566 or 415/276-9888; mandarinoriental. com; doubles from $$.

Ritz-Carlton (*89.98*) This elegant 336-room Nob Hill hotel has rain showers and 400-thread-count sheets. 600 Stockton St.; 800/241-3333 or 415/296-7465; ritzcarlton. com; doubles from $$.

St. Regis (*88.22*) In a 40-floor high-rise adjacent to the San Francisco Museum of Modern Art, with butlers for each floor. 125 3rd St.; 877/787-3447 or 415/284-4000; stregis.com; doubles from $$$.

SANTA BARBARA
Four Seasons Resort The Biltmore (*88.53*) A 207-room, clay-tiled-roof resort surrounded by palm trees. Guests have access to the members-only beach club. 800/332-3442 or 805/969-2261; fourseasons. com; doubles from $$$.

San Ysidro Ranch, A Rosewood Resort (*96.17*) On 500 bucolic

acres, clapboard cottages for just 90 guests that recently underwent a $150 million renovation. 888/767-3966 or 805/565-1700; rosewood hotels.com; doubles from $$$.

COLORADO
ASPEN
Little Nell (*91.78*) Aspen's only ski-in/ski-out property has adventure specialists and revamped rooms by designer Holly Hunt. 888/843-6355 or 970/920-4600; thelittlenell.com; doubles from $$$$.

St. Regis Aspen Resort (*87.47*) A 179-room brick hotel between Aspen Mountain's two main ski lifts. Suites come with butlers that provide unparalleled service. 877/787-3447 or 970/920-3300; stregisaspen.com; doubles from $$$.

BEAVER CREEK
Park Hyatt Resort & Spa (*86.77*) A 190-room lodge with stone-and-timber accents at the base of Beaver Creek Mountain that's known for its 30,000-square-foot spa. 877/875-4658 or 970/949-1234; park.hyatt. com; doubles from $$.

Ritz-Carlton, Bachelor Gulch (*89.58*) Gabled-roof lodge on Beaver Creek Mountain with a staff of ski concierges and a wellness roster that includes yoga. 800/241-3333 or 970/748-6200; ritzcarlton.com; doubles from $$$.

COLORADO SPRINGS
The Broadmoor (*89.57*) This 1918 lakeside Rocky Mountain mainstay is set on 3,000 acres; off-property excursions include horseback riding, rock climbing, and fly-fishing. 866/837-9520 or 719/577-5775; broadmoor.com; doubles from $$.

DENVER
Hotel Teatro (*86.71*) Renaissance Revival building across from the

Denver Center for the Performing Arts. 1100 14th St.; 888/727-1200 or 303/228-1100; hotelteatro.com; doubles from $.

Ritz-Carlton (*86.22*) Denver's toniest address: 202 spacious rooms and a steak house named after Broncos quarterback John Elway. 1881 Curtis St.; 800/241-3333 or 303/312-3800; ritzcarlton.com; doubles from $$.

VAIL
Sonnenalp Resort (*92.52*) A Bavarian-style lodge—awarded Sustainable Travel International LECS certification—with 112 ornate suites. 800/654-8312 or 970/476-5656; sonnenalp.com; doubles from $$$, including breakfast.

Vail Cascade Resort & Spa (*86.61*) A 292-room hotel with a new infinity pool, its own lift, and outdoor activities such as fly-fishing. 800/282-4183 or 970/476-7111; vailcascade.com; doubles from $$.

CONNECTICUT
WASHINGTON
Mayflower Inn & Spa (*90.44*) 30 rooms and a 20,000-square-foot spa in a stately English country–style inn on 58 acres in the Litchfield Hills. 860/868-9466; mayflowerinn. com; doubles from $$$.

DISTRICT OF COLUMBIA
WASHINGTON, D.C.
Four Seasons Hotel (*88.44*) Red-brick Georgetown stalwart with a well-edited art collection and iPads and Kindles for guest use. 2800 Pennsylvania Ave. NW; 800/332-3442 or 202/342-0444; fourseasons. com; doubles from $$$.

The Hay-Adams (*87.63*) A 1928 Italian Renaissance grande dame across from the White House. 16th and H Sts. NW; 800/853-6807 or

202/638-6600; hayadams.com; doubles from $$.

The Jefferson (*87.77*) Beaux-Arts landmark reopened with modern amenities (seating areas in lieu of a formal front desk; glass-roofed atriums) after a two-year renovation. 1200 16th St. NW; 202/347-2200; jeffersondc.com; doubles from $$$.

Ritz-Carlton Georgetown (*87.33*) Updated technology (new HD flat-screen televisions; iPod docking stations) in a National Historic Landmark. 3100 South St. NW; 800/241-3333 or 202/912-4100; ritzcarlton.com; doubles from $$.

Sofitel Washington D.C. Lafayette Square (*91.72*) Art Deco icon recently renovated by Pierre-Yves Rochon, with original gold-leaf details intact and a restaurant that sources local produce. 806 15th St. NW; 800/763-4835 or 202/730-8800; sofitel.com; doubles from $.

St. Regis (*88.15*) Stately 1926 hotel near the White House, with a new Alain Ducasse restaurant designed by David Rockwell, and an in-hotel historian. 16th and K Sts. NW; 877/787-3447 or 202/638-2626; stregis.com; doubles from $$$$.

FLORIDA
AMELIA ISLAND
Ritz-Carlton (*89.52*) On a quiet barrier island, 444 rooms (all with balconies) and a roster of activities. 800/241-3333 or 904/277-1100; ritzcarlton.com; doubles from $$.

CLEARWATER BEACH
Sandpearl Resort (*89.30*) A 253-room LEED Silver–certified property. The educational program includes tours of the Clearwater Marine Aquarium and a local artists-in-residence initiative. 877/726-3111

or 727/441-2425; sandpearl.com; doubles from $$.

FLORIDA KEYS

Little Palm Island Resort & Spa *(92.97)* Thatched-roof bungalows and a new Chef's Table, accessible by boat or seaplane from the mainland. Little Torch Key; 800/343-8567 or 305/872-2524; littlepalmisland.com; doubles from $$$$.

Marquesa Hotel *(88.94)* Group of 1884 clapboard houses set back from busy Duval Street. A no-cell-phones-in-public-spaces policy helps to keep the peace. Key West; 800/869-4631 or 305/292-1919; marquesa.com; doubles from $$.

Sunset Key Guest Cottages, a Westin Resort *(88.55)* White-washed cottages—with a new spa and restaurant—on a secluded island near Key West. Sunset Key; 800/228-3000; westin.com; doubles from $$$, including breakfast.

FORT LAUDERDALE

Atlantic Resort & Spa *(88.73)* Popular with families for its 600-square-foot-or-larger rooms furnished with kitchenettes. 877/567-8020 or 954/567-8020; atlantichotelfl.com; doubles from $$.

MIAMI AREA

Biltmore Hotel *(87.10)* A 1920's hotel surrounded by 150 manicured acres. The 270 rooms feature Frette robes and Egyptian-cotton sheets; the champagne brunch is legendary. Coral Gables; 800/727-1926 or 305/445-1926; biltmorehotel.com; doubles from $$.

Four Seasons Hotel *(87.87)* Housed in the 20th through 29th floors of a gleaming 70-story high-rise in Miami's financial district, 221 rooms with marble baths. 1435 Brickell Ave., Miami; 800/332-3442 or 305/358-3535; fourseasons.com; doubles from $$.

Mandarin Oriental *(87.64)* Newly renovated high-rise with a private beach, on Brickell Key. 500 Brickell Key Dr., Miami; 866/888-6780 or 305/913-8288; mandarinoriental.com; doubles from $$.

Ritz-Carlton, Key Biscayne *(88.11)* Family-friendly compound with 440 rooms in tropical colors, four restaurants, and 11 tennis courts, on a barrier island south of Miami Beach. Key Biscayne; 800/241-3333 or 305/365-4500; ritzcarlton.com; doubles from $$.

Ritz-Carlton, South Beach *(86.80)* On the beach, two poolside wings have 416 Art Deco rooms and a multimillion-dollar art collection. 1 Lincoln Rd., Miami Beach; 800/241-3333 or 786/276-4000; ritzcarlton.com; doubles from $$.

W South Beach *(86.44)* The 332 French-bohemian rooms (all with balconies) are appointed with photos by Danny Clinch. There's also the Bliss spa. 2201 Collins Ave., Miami; 877/946-8357; whotels.com; doubles from $$$$.

NAPLES

Ritz-Carlton *(90.10)* A 450-room complex (including two pools, a 51,000-square-foot spa, and a new small-plates restaurant) set along the Gulf of Mexico's Paradise Coast. 800/241-3333 or 239/598-3300; ritzcarlton.com; doubles from $$$.

Ritz-Carlton Golf Resort *(89.46)* The 295 elegant rooms join two Greg Norman–designed courses that double as an Audubon sanctuary, plus five restaurants. 800/241-3333 or 239/593-2000; ritzcarlton.com; doubles from $$.

Climbing gardens at San Ysidro Ranch, in Santa Barbara, California.

ORLANDO AREA

Disney's Animal Kingdom Lodge *(87.32)* A 972-room lodge within the Animal Kingdom theme park, offering lobbyside wildlife spotting. Lake Buena Vista; 407/934-7639; disneyworld.disney.go.com; doubles from $$.

Disney's Boardwalk Inn & Villas *(87.96)* A 904-room lakeside spread with 9,000 square feet of dining and shopping. Lake Buena Vista; 407/934-7639; disneyworld.disney.go.com; doubles from $$$.

Disney's Grand Floridian Resort & Spa *(88.64)* The empire's flagship: six red-roofed buildings set along the park's monorail loop. Lake Buena Vista; 407/934-7639; disneyworld.disney.go.com; doubles from $$$.

Disney's Wilderness Lodge *(86.81)* A 727-room behemoth with Western-inspired décor and a seven-story lobby in the Magic Kingdom. Lake Buena Vista; 407/934-7639; disneyworld.disney.go.com; doubles from $$.

Ritz-Carlton Orlando, Grande Lakes *(87.83)* An Italianate tower surrounded by lakes, trees, and a Greg Norman–designed golf course. 4012 Central Florida Pkwy., Orlando; 800/241-3333 or 407/206-2400; ritzcarlton.com; doubles from $$.

Sunbathers along the Royal Hawaiian's white-sand shore.

Villas of Grand Cypress (88.00) A hotel with 146 suites, Jack Nicklaus Signature courses, and a golf academy. 1 North Jacaranda, Orlando; 877/330-7377 or 407/239-4700; grandcypress.com; doubles from $$.

PALM BEACH
Brazilian Court Hotel & Beach Club (90.00) The 1926 hotel updated its Colonial-style interiors three years ago to the tune of $35 million and added a Daniel Boulud restaurant. 800/552-0335 or 561/655-7740; thebrazilian court.com; doubles from $$$.

The Breakers (89.95) Beachfront Italian Renaissance icon with a culinary focus. A $250 million renovation, to be completed in 2011, will add space to its 540 rooms. 888/273-2537 or 561/655-6611; thebreakers.com; doubles from $$.

Four Seasons Resort (87.00) Low-rise beachfront property with an old-world feel, plus a new 10,000-square-foot spa, 15 minutes from downtown. 800/332-3442 or 561/582-2800; fourseasons.com; doubles from $$.

PONTE VEDRA BEACH
Lodge & Club at Ponte Vedra Beach (86.22) Spanish colonial–inspired resort on a barrier island; the high staff-to-guest ratio ensures an intimate experience. 800/243-4304 or 904/273-9500; pvresorts.com; doubles from $$.

Ponte Vedra Inn & Club (89.62) A hotel for sporty types; the 26 rooms at the Summer House were just refurbished, but the golf-and-tennis center remains the top attraction. 800/234-7842 or 904/285-1111; pontevedra.com; doubles from $.

SANTA ROSA BEACH
WaterColor Inn & Resort (88.50) Urbanist enclave made up of a David Rockwell–designed inn and rental residences near a coastal dune lake. 866/426-2656 or 850/534-5000; watercolorresort.com; doubles from $$, including breakfast.

SARASOTA
Ritz-Carlton (88.94) An 18-story tower on Sarasita Bay, illuminated by crystal chandeliers and offering access to a private beach club on neighboring Lido Key. 800/241-3333 or 941/309-2000; ritzcarlton.com; doubles from $$.

GEORGIA
ATLANTA
Four Seasons Hotel (87.54) The first 19 floors of a 53-story building, within walking distance of the Atlanta Symphony. 75 14th St.; 800/332-3442 or 404/881-9898; fourseasons.com; doubles from $$.

InterContinental Buckhead (86.67) Business hotel that offers luxury amenities in Atlanta's upscale Buckhead neighborhood. 3315 Peachtree Rd. N.E.; 800/327-0200 or 404/946-4000; intercontinental.com; doubles from $.

Ritz-Carlton (87.09) Elegant 444-room structure (marble bathrooms; a chic new Lumen lobby bar) in the heart of downtown Atlanta. 181 Peachtree St. N.E.; 800/241-3333 or 404/659-0400; ritzcarlton.com; doubles from $$.

Ritz-Carlton, Buckhead (87.14) A 517-room high-rise suited for fitness buffs, across from high-end shopping. 3434 Peachtree Rd. N.E.; 800/241-3333 or 404/237-2700; ritzcarlton.com; doubles from $$.

GREENSBORO
Ritz-Carlton Lodge, Reynolds Plantation (87.70) Lakefront resort lauded for 99 holes of championship golf and the recently reopened Linger Longer Steakhouse. 800/241-3333 or 706/467-0600; ritzcarlton.com; doubles from $$.

SAVANNAH
Mansion on Forsyth Park (88.16) A 126-room hotel built alongside an 1888 mansion, with a low-country restaurant. 888/711-5114 or 912/238-5158; mansiononforsythpark.com; doubles from $.

SEA ISLAND
The Cloister (90.55) A historic 1928 Mediterranean-style mansion with

four pools, set on a secluded beach. 888/732-4752 or 912/638-3611; seaisland.com; doubles from $$.

Lodge at Sea Island Golf Club (91.00) Lodge with 40 country-style rooms and on-site access to a legendary golf course. A bagpiper roams the grounds every evening. 888/732-4752 or 912/638-3611; seaisland.com; doubles from $$.

HAWAII
BIG ISLAND
Four Seasons Resort Hualalai (92.74) Two-story bungalows built upon ancient lava rock. The updated Hualalai Spa now has 10 outdoor treatment rooms. 800/332-3442 or 808/325-8000; fourseasons.com; doubles from $$$$.

Mauna Kea Beach Hotel (87.47) Golf-and-tennis resort on Kaunaoa Beach, with new interiors after a $150 million renovation. 866/977-4589 or 808/882-7222; princeresorts hawaii.com; doubles from $$.

Mauna Lani Bay Hotel & Bungalows (88.96) A 343-room eco-friendly hotel on a 16th-century lava flow, the current nesting ground of eight endangered sea turtles. 800/367-2323 or 808/885-6622; maunalani.com; doubles from $$.

KAUAI
Grand Hyatt Kauai Resort & Spa (88.41) Sprawling 602-room resort with a network of pools and a cliff-top Robert Trent Jones Jr.–designed golf course. 800/233-1234 or 808/742-1234; hyatt.com; doubles from $$$.

LANAI
Four Seasons Resort Lanai at Manele Bay (89.52) A 236-room beach resort fronted by a marine preserve. Pool attendants give hand massages to vacationing urbanites with texting-weary fingers. 800/332-

3442 or 808/565-2000; fourseasons. com; doubles from $$.

Four Seasons Resort Lanai, The Lodge at Koele (91.39) Manele Bay's tiled sister property, complete with English gardens and a horse stable. 800/332-3442 or 808/565-4000; fourseasons.com; doubles from $$.

MAUI
Fairmont Kea Lani (87.69) Whitewashed all-suite retreat on Polo Beach maintains an air of tranquillity despite its size. Rooms were just spruced up with new furnishings. 800/441-1414; fairmont. com; doubles from $$.

Four Seasons Resort Maui at Wailea (89.91) This 380-room retreat has an underwater sound system in its infinity pool and offers a slew of free activities. 800/332-3442 or 808/874-8000; fourseasons. com; doubles from $$.

Hotel Hana-Maui & Honua Spa (88.64) This collection of 47 cottages and 22 suites on a seaside bluff is a quiet alternative to the island's mega-resorts. 800/321-4262 or 808/248-8211; hotelhanamaui.com; doubles from $$.

Hyatt Regency Maui Resort & Spa (87.20) Upscale resort with Polynesian-inspired design, renovated rooms, and a new Asian-fusion restaurant, Japengo, on the northwest side of the island. 800/233-1234 or 808/661-1234; hyatt.com; doubles from $$.

Makena Beach & Golf Resort (86.67) Low-key hotel on 1,800 acres abutting a crescent of white sand. New this year: the Makena Kai Day Spa and a seafood-focused restaurant. 800/321-6284 or 808/874-1111; makenaresortmaui. com; doubles from $$.

Ritz-Carlton, Kapalua (87.49) Former pineapple plantation known for its eco-education program. Updated guest rooms have dark-wood floors and watercolor paintings. 800/241-3333 or 808/669-6200; ritzcarlton.com; doubles from $$$.

OAHU
Halekulani (92.43) Century-old, Waikiki Beach gem with tech-savvy details and a new restaurant—plus covetable views of Diamond Head. 800/367-2343 or 808/923-2311; halekulani.com; doubles from $$.

Kahala Hotel & Resort (91.53) A 338-room Hawaiian classic with furniture by notable designers (Nicole Miller; Ralph Lauren) in refurbished suites. 800/367-2525 or 808/739-8888; kahalaresort.com; doubles from $$$.

Royal Hawaiian, a Luxury Collection Resort (87.41) After a $60 million renovation, the famous pink hotel has 529 updated rooms and an intimate new pool. 800/325-3589 or 808/923-7311; royalhawaiian. com; doubles from $$$.

ILLINOIS
CHICAGO
The Drake (86.67) A storied history and 535 rooms and suites with Regency-style furnishings. 140 E. Walton Place; 800/553-7253 or 312/787-2200; thedrakehotel.com; doubles from $.

Four Seasons Hotel (91.77) Floors 30 through 46 of a skyscraper overlooking Lake Michigan, with a mix of 20th-century French design and Art Deco details. 120 E. Delaware Place; 800/332-3442 or 312/280-8800; fourseasons.com; doubles from $$.

Park Hyatt (87.80) A 198-room hotel on Water Tower Square, with a

modern art collection (including works by Isamu Noguchi) and views of the lake. 800 N. Michigan Ave.; 877/875-4658 or 312/335-1234; park.hyatt.com; doubles from $$.

Peninsula Chicago (93.09) Sleek 20-story tower and two of the city's hottest restaurants, Avenues and Shanghai Terrace, in the heart of the Magnificent Mile. 108 E. Superior St.; 866/382-8388 or 312/337-2888; peninsula.com; doubles from $$.

Ritz-Carlton (A Four Seasons Hotel) (89.12) Lavish 21-floor Magnificent Mile high-rise hotel. The renovated lobby features a marble fountain and Art Nouveau–style reliefs. 160 E. Pearson St.; 800/332-3442 or 312/266-1000; fourseasons.com; doubles from $$.

Sofitel Water Tower (88.38) Sofitel's North American flagship is a 32-floor light-filled glass prism, with a new Parisian-inspired restaurant. 20 E. Chestnut St.; 800/763-4835 or 312/324-4000; sofitel.com; doubles from $.

Sutton Place Hotel (92.27) A 246-room contemporary tower on the Gold Coast, near luxe boutiques and top dining options. 21 E. Bellevue Place; 866/378-8866 or 312/266-2100; suttonplace.com; doubles from $$.

Swissôtel (86.58) Swiss efficiency in downtown Chicago, with a new 38,000-square-foot event center. 323 E. Wacker Dr.; 888/737-9477 or 312/565-0565; swissotelchicago. com; doubles from $.

Trump International Hotel & Tower (94.32) Located in a minimalist, 92-story stainless-steel monolith next to the Chicago River, with a 23,000 square-foot spa. 401 N. Wabash Ave.; 877/458-7867 or 312/588-8000; trumpchicago hotel.com; doubles from $$.

KENTUCKY
LOUISVILLE
21c Museum Hotel (89.60) In a 19th-century building, 90 industrial rooms and a multi-million dollar art collection. 877/217-6400 or 502/217-6300; 21cmuseumhotel. com; doubles from $.

LOUISIANA
NEW ORLEANS
Ritz-Carlton (86.91) Converted department store located one block from Bourbon Street. Post-Katrina, the hotel underwent a $150 million renovation. 921 Canal St.; 800/241-3333 or 504/524-1331; ritzcarlton. com; doubles from $$.

Windsor Court Hotel (88.84) Near the French Quarter, 322 traditional accommodations—mostly suites—with bay windows. 300 Gravier St.; 888/596-0955 or 504/523-6000; windsorcourthotel. com; doubles from $.

MAINE
CAPE ELIZABETH
Inn by the Sea (86.89) This five-acre resort—connected by board-walk to Crescent Beach—reopened in June 2008 after green-focused renovations. 800/888-4287 or 207/799-3134; innbythesea.com; doubles from $$.

KENNEBUNKPORT
White Barn Inn (89.86) A collection of 19th-century buildings furnished with sleigh beds and rain showers. The namesake restaurant updates its four-course prix fixe menu weekly. 800/735-2478; whitebarninn.com; doubles from $$, including breakfast.

MARYLAND
ST. MICHAELS
Inn at Perry Cabin (88.32) Colonial-style 1816 manor—a classic Eastern Shore inn—on a private Chesapeake Bay inlet. 866/278-9601 or 410/745-2200; perrycabin.com; doubles from $$.

MASSACHUSETTS
BOSTON AREA
Charles Hotel (86.53) Harvard Square hotel with a New England aesthetic (Shaker-inspired furniture; geometric quilts) and two excellent restaurants. One Bennett St., Cambridge; 800/882-1818 or 617/864-1200; charleshotel.com; doubles from $$.

Eliot Hotel (90.15) Elegant Back Bay hotel—family-owned for 50 years. Bathrooms are being updated with Bardiglio Italian marble. 370 Commonwealth Ave.; 800/443-5468 or 617/267-1607; eliothotel.com; doubles from $$.

Four Seasons Hotel (88.83) A 273-room brick landmark, across the street from the walking paths of the Boston Common (Newbury Street's shops are also just a few blocks away). 200 Boylston St.; 800/332-3442 or 617/338-4400; fourseasons. com; doubles from $$$.

Hotel Commonwealth (90.59) Tech-savvy French Empire–style property next to Fenway Park. New additions include the Baseball Suite and Island Creek Oyster Bar. 500 Commonwealth Ave.; 866/784-4000 or 617/933-5000; hotel commonwealth.com; doubles from $$.

The Taj (88.00) Legendary 1927 hotel (formerly the flagship Ritz-Carlton) beside the Public Garden. 15 Arlington St.; 866/969-1825 or 617/536-5700; tajhotels.com; doubles from $.

XV Beacon (87.71) Cozy 60-room boutique hotel with bold décor that contrasts nicely with its 1903 Beaux-Arts exterior. All rooms have fireplaces. 15 Beacon St.; 877/982-3226 or 617/670-1500; xvbeacon. com; doubles from $$.

CAPE COD
Wequassett Resort & Golf Club (88.00) On a sailboat-filled bay, with a 1740's Colonial reception area, recently renovated rooms in clapboard cottages, and 29 acres of gardens. Chatham; 800/225-7125 or 508/432-5400; wequassett.com; doubles from $$$.

NANTUCKET
White Elephant (88.50) Nantucket Town's largest resort, with chaise-dotted lawns, a waterfront patio, and updated one- and two-bedroom Garden cottages. 800/445-6574 or 508/228-2500; whiteelephanthotel. com; doubles from $$$.

MICHIGAN
BAY HARBOR
Inn at Bay Harbor (86.86) Traditional Victorian resort along Lake Michigan's Little Traverse Bay, with three Arthur Hills–designed courses. 800/462-6963 or 231/439-4000; innatbayharbor.com; doubles from $$.

BIRMINGHAM
Townsend Hotel (90.26) In a gilded Detroit suburb that's convenient to the city, 150 rooms (three with four-poster beds and full kitchens) with marble baths. 800/548-4172 or 248/642-7900; townsendhotel.com; doubles from $$.

MACKINAC ISLAND
Grand Hotel (86.36) A grand retreat built in 1887, with one of the world's greatest front porches. 800/334-7263 or 906/847-3331; grandhotel.com; doubles from $$, including breakfast and dinner.

MINNESOTA
MINNEAPOLIS
Graves 601 Hotel (87.00) Within walking distance of restaurants, theaters, and the Twins' new stadium, 255 modern rooms. 601 1st Ave. N.; 866/523-1100 or 612/677-1100; graves601hotel.com; doubles from $.

MISSOURI
KANSAS CITY
Raphael Hotel (88.80) A 1920's European-style property overlooking Country Club Plaza, the first suburban outdoor shopping center in the U.S. 325 Ward Pkwy.; 800/821-5343 or 816/756-3800; raphaelkc.com; doubles from $.

ST. LOUIS
Four Seasons Hotel (89.83) A 200-room hotel with streamlined interiors in a convenient downtown location, near the Gateway Arch. 999 N. 2nd St.; 800/332-3442 or 314/ 881-5800; fourseasons.com; doubles from $.

Ritz-Carlton (86.74) An 18-story hotel in an upscale residential enclave. A $14 million renovation was completed last year. 100 Carondelet Plaza; 800/241-3333 or 314/863-6300; ritzcarlton.com; doubles from $.

MONTANA
DARBY
Triple Creek Ranch (96.76) Adults-only mountain retreat on thousands of acres with recently refreshed log

cabins (wood-burning fireplaces; hot tubs). 800/654-2943 or 406/821-4600; triplecreekranch.com; doubles from $$$$, all-inclusive.

NEVADA
LAS VEGAS AREA

Bellagio *(88.89)* A mid-Strip extravaganza with a 55,000-square-foot spa, 14 restaurants, and dancing fountains. 3600 Las Vegas Blvd. S.; 888/987-6667 or 702/693-7111; bellagio.com; doubles from $.

Encore at Wynn *(88.52)* Steve Wynn's latest resort feels like a desert oasis; the new Encore Beach Club has three tiered pools and 40-foot palm trees. 3131 Las Vegas Blvd. S.; 888/320-7125 or 702/770-8000; encorelasvegas.com; doubles from $.

Four Seasons Hotel *(88.64)* A tranquil spot on the strip's southern tip, with plush room amenities and no casino. 3960 Las Vegas Blvd. S.; 800/332-3442 or 702/632-5000; fourseasons.com; doubles from $.

Loews Lake *(87.06)* Child- and pet-friendly resort on the lake, plus watersports galore, and a 9,000-square-foot spa. 101 Montelago Blvd., Henderson; 866/262-4280 or 702/567-6000; loewshotels.com; doubles from $.

The Palazzo *(89.94)* All-suite property with over-the-top room décor, a two-story fountain in the entry, a Barneys New York, and a Canyon Ranch SpaClub. 3325 Las Vegas Blvd. S.; 877/883-6423 or 702/607-4100; palazzolasvegas.com; doubles from $.

Venetian Resort Hotel Casino *(88.37)* A condensed version of its namesake city, with some of the Strip's largest rooms and Wolfgang Puck's Postrio Bar & Grill. It was just LEED Gold certified. 3355 Las Vegas

Blvd. S.; 866/659-9643 or 702/414-1000; venetian.com; doubles from $.

Wynn Las Vegas *(89.68)* The flagship property from developer Steve Wynn has 2,716 rooms, plus restaurants overseen by up-and-coming celebrity chefs. 3131 Las Vegas Blvd. S.; 877/321-9966 or 702/770-7000; wynnlasvegas.com; doubles from $.

NEW HAMPSHIRE
NEW CASTLE

Wentworth by the Sea, a Marriott Hotel & Spa *(88.30)* Meticulously restored 1874 grand hotel, on an Atlantic Ocean island just an hour north of Boston. 800/228-9290 or 603/422-7322; wentworth.com; doubles from $$.

NEW MEXICO
SANTA FE

Rosewood Inn of the Anasazi *(90.15)* A 58-room boutique property with Native American–style design, steps from historic Santa Fe Plaza. 113 Washington Ave.; 888/767-3966 or 505/988-3030; innoftheanasazi.com; doubles from $.

NEW YORK
ADIRONDACKS

Mirror Lake Inn Resort & Spa *(89.71)* Family-friendly compound with a range of outdoor activities (hiking; fishing; dog-sledding), just a block from downtown Lake Placid. Lake Placid; 518/523-2544; mirrorlakeinn.com; doubles from $$.

Whiteface Lodge *(91.25)* Rustic, all-suite lodge featuring cast-iron fireplaces and full kitchens, abutting the six million-acre Adirondack Park. Lake Placid; 800/903-4045 or 518/523-0500; thewhitefacelodge.com; doubles from $$$.

FINGER LAKES

Mirbeau Inn & Spa *(89.25)* An extravagant take on a French country

estate, located on 10 wooded acres within a quaint village. There are four guest cottages and Monet-inspired gardens. Skaneateles; 877/647-2328 or 315/685-1927; mirbeau.com; doubles from $$.

NEW YORK CITY

Four Seasons Hotel *(89.36)* Soaring I. M. Pei–designed tower with outstanding views of midtown skyscrapers and rooms that average 600 square feet. 57 E. 57th St.; 800/332-3442 or 212/758-5700; fourseasons.com; doubles from $$$$$.

London NYC *(86.34)* Elegant midtown hotel composed almost entirely of suites; best known for Gordon Ramsay's restaurant. 151 W. 54th St.; 888/566-3692 or 212/307-5000; thelondonnyc.com; doubles from $$.

Mandarin Oriental *(88.26)* On the 35th through 54th floors of the Time Warner building on Columbus Circle, with a noteworthy spa. 80 Columbus Circle; 866/801-8880 or 212/805-8800; mandarinoriental.com; doubles from $$$.

Pierre Gonnord's *Nico,* hanging in a guest room at 21c Museum Hotel, in Louisville, Kentucky.

Castle Hill Inn's Agassiz
Mansion, with its Turret Suite,
in Newport, Rhode Island.

New York Palace (*86.20*)
Dorchester Collection's 19th-century
mansion and 55-story building in
midtown. The Towers floors
reopened in September 2010. 455
Madison Ave.; 800/804-7035 or
212/888-7000; newyorkpalace.com;
doubles from $$$$$.

Peninsula New York (*90.05*)
Classic Beaux-Arts façade and
a refurbished modern interior,
near midtown shopping. 700
5th Ave.; 866/382-8388 or
212/956-2888; peninsula.com;
doubles from $$$$.

The Plaza (*89.60*) This landmark
luxury hotel reopened in 2008 after
extensive renovations that added a
spa and the Food Hall by Todd
English. 5th Ave. at Central Park S.;
800/441-1414 or 212/759-3000;
theplaza.com; doubles from $$$$$.

Ritz-Carlton Central Park (*92.17*)
A 33-story limestone tower on
Central Park. 50 Central Park S.;
800/241-3333 or 212/308-9100; ritz
carlton.com; doubles from $$$$

St. Regis (*90.97*) The 1904 Beaux-
Arts icon on Fifth Avenue houses
Alain Ducasse's Adour restaurant
and features luxurious Waterford
crystal chandeliers. 2 E. 55th St.;
877/787-3447 or 212/753-4500;
stregis.com; doubles from $$$$.

**Trump International Hotel &
Tower** (*89.58*) The Donald's glass
monolith on Central Park has one
of the city's top restaurants, Jean
Georges. A multimillion-dollar
renovation was completed in 2010.
1 Central Park W.; 888/448-7867
or 212/299-1000; trumpintl.com;
doubles from $$$.

NORTH CAROLINA
ASHEVILLE
Inn on Biltmore Estate (*90.76*) A
210-room mansion set on 8,000 acres
on George Vanderbilt's Biltmore
estate, surrounded by the Blue Ridge
Mountains. 800/411-3812 or 828/225-
1600; biltmore.com; doubles from $$.

CARY
Umstead Hotel & Spa (*88.80*)
Tranquil 150-room property on 12
wooded acres, minutes from
downtown Raleigh. 866/877-4141 or
919/447-4000; theumstead.com;
doubles from $$.

PITTSBORO
Fearrington House Country Inn
(*92.47*) 32-room inn with manicured
gardens, a restaurant set in a 1927
farmhouse, and, in fall 2011, a
bi-level spa—8 miles from Chapel
Hill. 800/735-2478 or 919/542-2121;
fearrington.com; doubles from $$.

OHIO
CLEVELAND
Ritz-Carlton (*88.53*) A 205-room
tower overlooking Lake Erie, within
walking distance of the Historic
Warehouse District. 1515 W. 3rd St.;
800/241-3333 or 216/623-1300;
ritzcarlton.com; doubles from $$.

OREGON
CANNON BEACH
Stephanie Inn Hotel (*89.12*)
Shingled sanctuary overlooking
Haystack Rock. The 41 rooms are
equipped with fireplaces and private
balconies. 800/633-3466 or 503/436-
2221; stephanie-inn.com; doubles
from $$, including breakfast.

PORTLAND
**The Nines, a Luxury Collection
Hotel** (*89.29*) A 331-room LEED
Silver–certified hotel within the top
floors of the landmark Meier &
Frank department store building.
525 S.W. Morrison St.; 800/325-
3589; thenines.com; doubles from $.

PENNSYLVANIA
BEDFORD
Omni Bedford Springs Resort
(*87.62*) Sprawling 2,200-acre
getaway (with a brick-and-white-
column façade, 216 rooms, and two
pools), just outside of town.
888/444-6664 or 814/623-8100;
omnihotels.com; doubles from $.

PHILADELPHIA
Four Seasons Hotel (*88.37*) Eight-
story granite hotel with a central
location—plus Philly's best spa. One
Logan Square; 800/332-3442 or
215/963-1500; fourseasons.com;
doubles from $$.

Loews Hotel (*86.67*) Housed in a
1932 former bank building, minutes
from the Amtrak station. 1200
Market St.; 866/563-9792 or
215/627-1200; loewshotels.com;
doubles from $.

Rittenhouse Hotel (*92.97*)
Prestigious address on Rittenhouse
Square, unbeatable service, and
98 large rooms. Public spaces
display paintings by Mary Cassatt.
210 W. Rittenhouse Square;
800/635-1042 or 215/546-9000;
rittenhousehotel.com; doubles
from $$$.

RHODE ISLAND
NEWPORT
Castle Hill Inn (*89.20*) 19th-century
Victorian mansion on a peninsula
where the Atlantic meets Narragansett

Bay. 888/466-1355 or 401/849-3800; castlehillinn.com; doubles from $$$$, including breakfast.

SOUTH CAROLINA
BLUFFTON
Inn at Palmetto Bluff, an Auberge Resort (93.43) Southern-style resort on coastal marshland, with 50 cottage rooms, spa treatments, and outdoor activities. 866/706-6565 or 843/706-6500; palmettobluffresort. com; doubles from $$.

SUMMERVILLE
Woodlands Inn (94.12) Neo-Georgian mansion from 1906 with touches of Tara; a bastion of Southern hospitality. 800/774-9999 or 843/875-2600; woodlandsinn. com; doubles from $.

CHARLESTON
Charleston Place (90.68) One of the city's larger and most luxurious hotels, with a 1-to-2 staff-to-guest ratio. 205 Meeting St.; 888/635-2350 or 843/722-4900; charlestonplace. com; doubles from $$.

Planters Inn (89.70) Peaceful 19th-century building and modern addition in the center of town. The 64 rooms have crown moldings and four-poster beds. 112 N. Market St.; 800/735-2478 or 843/722-2345; plantersinn.com; doubles from $$.

KIAWAH ISLAND
Sanctuary at Kiawah Island Golf Resort (89.09) Stately 255-room hotel on the grounds of one of the country's top golf resorts. 800/654-2924 or 843/768-2121; kiawahresort.com; doubles from $$.

TENNESSEE
NASHVILLE
Hermitage Hotel (90.91) The city's choicest digs—favored by country-music stars since 1910—looks fresh thanks to a $17 million overhaul.

231 6th Ave. N.; 888/888-9414 or 615/244-3121; thehermitagehotel. com; doubles from $$.

WALLAND
Blackberry Farm (91.46) Rural luxury at its best, with renowned cuisine and a cooking school, set on a farmstead in the Great Smoky Mountains. 800/273-6004 or 865/984-8166; black berryfarm.com; doubles from $$$$.

TEXAS
AUSTIN
Four Seasons Hotel (90.55) 291-room Southwestern-style structure on the green banks of Lady Bird Lake. 98 San Jacinto Blvd.; 800/332-3442 or 512/478-4500; fourseasons. com; doubles from $$.

DALLAS AREA
The Adolphus (91.48) Opened by beer magnate Adolphus Busch in 1912, this hotel has a roster of famous guests (Babe Ruth; Tom Hanks). 1321 Commerce St., Dallas; 800/221-9083 or 214/742-8200; hotel adolphus.com; doubles from $$.

Four Seasons Resort & Club at Las Colinas (86.42) Surrounded by 400 acres of North Texas hills, with 431 rooms and a spa. 4150 N. MacArthur Blvd., Irving; 800/332-3442 or 972/717-0700; fourseasons. com; doubles from $$.

Hotel ZaZa (88.90) A stylish French Mediterranean–inspired villa overlooking Uptown's McKinney Avenue. 2332 Leonard St., Dallas; 888/880-3244 or 214/468-8399; hotelzazadallas.com; doubles from $$.

Omni Mandalay Hotel at Las Colinas (86.93) Business-district hotel that features Burmese-style antiques and a heated lakeside pool. 221 E. Las Colinas Blvd., Irving; 888/444-6664 or 972/556-0800; omnihotels.com; doubles from $$.

Rosewood Crescent Hotel (89.48) In the Uptown neighborhood of Dallas, a limestone landmark with 220 modern rooms and a Nobu outpost. 400 Crescent Court, Dallas; 888/767-3966 or 214/871-3200; rose woodhotels.com; doubles from $$$.

Rosewood Mansion on Turtle Creek (92.28) This 143-room resort—a former cotton magnate's mansion—was recently refreshed for its 30th anniversary. 2821 Turtle Creek Blvd., Dallas; 888/767-3966 or 214/559-2100; mansiononturtlecreek. com; doubles from $$$.

HOUSTON
Houstonian Hotel, Club & Spa (91.51) Lodge-style hotel with an indoor tennis facility, set within an 18-acre pine forest. 111 N. Post Oak Lane; 800/231-2759 or 713/680-2626; houstonian.com; doubles from $$.

St. Regis (86.44) Texas-inspired hotel conveniently situated on a wooded lot near the Houston Galleria mall. Note the impressive flower arrangements. 1919 Briar Oaks Lane; 877/787-3447 or 713/840-7600; stregis.com; doubles from $$$.

SAN ANTONIO
Hotel Valencia Riverwalk (86.38) A 213-room palazzo on the River Walk, with striking interiors and a Mediterranean-style exterior. 150 E. Houston St.; 866/842-0100 or 210/227-9700; hotelvalencia-riverwalk.com; doubles from $$.

JW Marriott Hill Country Resort & Spa (87.20) Six-story resort in Texas Hill Country, 20 minutes from downtown San Antonio. 23808 Resort Pkwy.; 800/228-9290 or 210/276-2500; jwmarriott.com; doubles from $$.

Omni La Mansión del Rio (86.64) An 1852 former Spanish-colonial school building; now a 338-room hotel and courtyard with fountains along the Riverwalk. 112 College St.; 888/444-6664 or 210/518-1000; omnihotels.com; doubles from $.

Westin La Cantera Resort (86.90) Six pools, tennis courts, golf, and bird's eye views of the area's live oak groves in Texas Hill Country. 16641 La Cantera Pkwy.; 800/446-5387 or 210/558-6500; westinlacantera.com; doubles from $$.

UTAH
PARK CITY
Stein Eriksen Lodge (90.88) Timeless mid-mountain Norwegian-style chalet at Deer Valley ski resort. 800/453-1302 or 435/649-3700; steinlodge.com; doubles from $$$, including breakfast during ski season.

SALT LAKE CITY
Grand America Hotel (86.27) An opulent 24-story structure with handcrafted Richelieu furniture in the 775 guest rooms. 555 S. Main St.; 800/621-4505 or 801/258-6000; grandamerica.com; doubles from $.

VERMONT
STOWE
Topnotch Resort & Spa (88.18) The first full resort at Stowe, with a mega-spa that ensures après-ski pampering and an ideal location at the base of Vermont's tallest peak. 800/451-8686 or 802/253-8585; topnotchresort.com; doubles from $.

VIRGINIA
ARLINGTON
Ritz-Carlton, Pentagon City (*88.52*) On the Potomac River, 366 rooms (400-thread-count sheets; goose-down featherbeds) near D.C.'s major monuments. 1250 S. Hayes St.; 800/241-3333 or 703/415-5000; ritzcarlton.com; doubles from $$.

CHARLOTTESVILLE
Keswick Hall (*87.81*) Stately Tuscan-style structure dating from 1912, with decadent guest rooms (hunt-club prints; canopy beds; Chippendale chairs) and one of Virginia's top restaurants. 701 Club Dr.; 800/274-5391 or 434/979-3440; keswick.com; doubles from $$.

HOT SPRINGS
The Homestead (*86.87*) A 1766 grand brick property in Southern style, with three golf courses. The hotel recently renovated 157 rooms and suites. 800/838-1766 or 540/839-1766; thehomestead.com; doubles from $$.

MCLEAN
Ritz-Carlton, Tysons Corner (*88.93*) Contemporary tower with traditional interiors, across the Potomac from D.C. 800/241-3333 or 703/506-4300; ritzcarlton.com; doubles from $$.

RICHMOND
Jefferson Hotel (*87.38*) An 1895 Beaux-Arts property complete with porticoes and a clock tower. 101 W. Franklin St.; 800/424-8014 or 804/788-8000; jeffersonhotel.com; doubles from $$.

WASHINGTON
Inn at Little Washington (*88.25*) Romantic early-20th-century manor—a theatrical riot of fabrics and wallpapers. 540/675-3800; theinnatlittlewashington.com; doubles from $$.

WASHINGTON
SEATTLE
Alexis Hotel (*87.33*) Walls of this downtown boutique hotel display original art selected by a Seattle Art Museum curator. 1007 1st Ave.; 888/850-1155 or 206/624-4844; alexishotel.com; doubles from $$.

Fairmont Olympic Hotel (*86.32*) Over-the-top property exuding old-world glamour—a rarity in Seattle. 411 University St.; 800/441-1414 or 206/621-1700; fairmont.com; doubles from $$.

Four Seasons Hotel (*88.24*) Two-year-old, 21-story hotel with captivating views of Puget Sound. 99 Union St.; 800/332-3442 or 206/749-7000; fourseasons.com; doubles from $$.

Grand Hyatt (*87.29*) Sleek tower downtown, convenient to Pike Place Market and some of the city's best shopping. 721 Pine St.; 800/233-1234 or 206/774-1234; hyatt.com; doubles from $.

Hotel Monaco (*86.20*) A playful 11-story hotel: rooms boast theatrical prints; the lobby has an aquatic theme. 1101 4th Ave.; 800/715-6513 or 206/621-1770; monaco-seattle.com; doubles from $$.

Vintage Park (*87.25*) A 1922 brick structure downtown, with wood interiors that resemble a European inn. 1100 5th Ave.; 800/853-3914 or 206/624-8000; hotelvintagepark.com; doubles from $$.

WHIDBEY ISLAND
Inn at Langley (*87.56*) Intimate retreat on a Puget Sound island, with a weekends-only (plus Thursdays in summer) restaurant that's justly famous. Langley; 360/221-3033; innatlangley.com; doubles from $$, including breakfast.

WEST VIRGINIA
WHITE SULPHUR SPRINGS
The Greenbrier (*88.48*) Renovated 1913 resort in the Allegheny Mountains, known for its Dorothy Draper interiors. The new restaurant and casino complex was designed by Carleton Varney. 300 W. Main St.; 800/453-4858 or 304/536-1110; greenbrier.com; doubles from $.

WYOMING
JACKSON/GRAND TETON
Four Seasons Resort (*93.43*) A team of adventure concierges is at the ready at this ski-in, ski-out lodge. Teton Village; 800/332-3442 or 307/732-5000; fourseasons.com; doubles from $$$.

Rusty Parrot Lodge & Spa (*86.40*) A 31-room gabled lodgepole pine inn

Ancient Cedars Spa at British Columbia's Wickaninnish Inn.

near Jackson's town square, with excellent service (house-made cookies await returning skiers). 800/739-1749 or 307/733-2000; rustyparrot.com; doubles from $$.

Canada

ALBERTA

BANFF

Fairmont Banff Springs (87.26) A 19th-century Scottish castle amid the peaks of Banff National Park. 800/441-1414 or 403/762-2211; fairmont.com; doubles from $$.

LAKE LOUISE

Post Hotel & Spa (93.07) Chalet-style lodge with a 26,000-bottle wine cellar—one of Canada's largest. 800/661-1586 or 403/522-3989; posthotel.com; doubles from $$.

BRITISH COLUMBIA

TOFINO

Wickaninnish Inn (93.14) Nature- and food-focused inn on a rocky promontory, with Pacific Rim National Park as a backdrop. 800/333-4604 or 250/725-3100; wickinn.com; doubles from $$.

VANCOUVER

Pan Pacific (87.35) In downtown Vancouver, 503 waterfront rooms. 300-999 Canada Place; 877/324-4856 or 604/662-8111; panpacific.com; doubles from $.

VICTORIA

Fairmont Empress (87.69) Edwardian landmark overlooking Inner Harbour and known for its afternoon tea (served under a portrait of Queen Mary). 800/441-1414 or 250/384-8111; fairmont.com; doubles from $$.

WHISTLER

Fairmont Chateau Whistler (86.32) Ski-in, ski-out resort in the upper village, with a Robert Trent Jones Jr.–designed golf course and GPS-equipped golf carts. 800/441-1414 or 604/938-8000; fairmont.com; doubles from $$.

Four Seasons Resort (89.57) Stone-and-timber lodge with a new steak house, Sidecut, at the base of Blackcomb Mountain. 800/332-3442 or 604/935-3400; fourseasons.com; doubles from $$.

ONTARIO

TORONTO

Park Hyatt (87.33) In Yorkville—the epicenter of activity during the city's film festival—across from the Royal Ontario Museum. 4 Avenue Rd.; 877/875-4658 or 416/925-1234; park.hyatt.com; doubles from $$.

QUEBEC

QUEBEC CITY

Auberge Saint-Antoine (92.80) The 95 rooms—some with 300-year-old artifacts—sit on the St. Lawrence River. 8 Rue St.-Antoine; 888/692-2211 or 418/692-2211; saint-antoine.com; doubles from $$.

Fairmont Le Château Frontenac (87.51) Copper-roofed 1893 castle overlooking the St. Lawrence River in Old Quebec, with a just-opened Payot spa. 1 Rue des Carrières; 800/441-1414 or 418/692-3861; fairmont.com; doubles from $.

The Caribbean, Bermuda, & the Bahamas

ANGUILLA

Cap Juluca (86.39) This 95-room Greco-Moorish resort underwent a $22 million renovation in 2008. Maundays Bay; 888/858-5822 or 264/497-6779; capjuluca.com; doubles from $$$$, including breakfast.

CuisinArt Resort & Spa (86.76) Whitewashed villas on a cove, with the island's largest spa. Rendezvous Bay; 800/943-3210 or 264/498-2000; cuisinartresort.com; doubles from $$$$.

ANTIGUA

Curtain Bluff Resort (89.33) A 1950's beach house and renovated buildings on a rocky outpost; there's a weekly cocktail party for guests. St. John's; 888/289-9898 or 268/462-8400; curtainbluff.com; doubles from $$$$, all-inclusive.

BAHAMAS

One&Only Ocean Club (89.14) British-colonial plantation with a Jean-Georges Vongerichten restaurant. Paradise Island; 866/552-0001 or 242/363-2501; oneandonly resorts.com; doubles from $$$$.

BARBADOS

Sandy Lane (90.24) A Bentley airport transfer brings guests to this Palladian-style palace on a quiet bay. St. James; 866/444-4080 or 246/444-2001; sandylane.com; doubles from $$$$$, including breakfast.

BERMUDA

Reefs Hotel & Club (89.08) A 57-room property along Bermuda's southern coast. Southampton; 800/742-2008 or 441/238-0222; thereefs.com; doubles from $$$, including breakfast and dinner.

The cove at Tucker's Point Hotel & Spa, in Bermuda.

Tucker's Point Hotel & Spa
(90.59) 88-room British-colonial-style resort (mahogany beds; soaking tubs) on 200 pink-sand acres. Hamilton Parish; 866/604-3764 or 441/298-4000; tuckerspoint.com; doubles from $$$.

The lobby at Alvear Palace, in Buenos Aires.

BRITISH VIRGIN ISLANDS
TORTOLA
Peter Island Resort & Spa
(89.85) A 1,800-acre private island getaway with a 2-to-1 staff-to-guest ratio and five restaurants. Peter Island; 800/346-4451 or 284/495-2000; peterisland.com; doubles from $$$.

CAYMAN ISLANDS
Ritz-Carlton, Grand Cayman
(89.50) A 365-room oceanfront haven offering nature tours by Jean-Michel Cousteau. Seven Mile Beach; 800/241-3333 or 345/943-9000; ritz-carlton.com; doubles from $$.

JAMAICA
Couples Negril (88.41) An 18-acre retreat with five restaurants on Bloody Bay Beach with an underwater scuba resort. Negril; 800/268-7537 or 876/957-5960; couples.com; doubles from $$$, all-inclusive, three-night minimum.

Couples Sans Souci (91.00) Adults-only resort and spa in a seaside cove. Ocho Rios; 800/268-7537 or 876/994-1206; couples.com; doubles from $$$, all-inclusive, three-night minimum.

Couples Swept Away (91.38) A 27-acre all-suite hideaway with a fitness complex. Westmoreland; 800/268-7537 or 876/957-4061; couples.com; doubles from $$$$, all-inclusive, three-night minimum.

Couples Tower Isle (92.47) A 226-room resort—the hotel chain's first—with an award-winning spa. Ocho Rios; 800/268-7537 or 876/975-4271; couples.com; doubles from $$$, all-inclusive, three-night minimum.

Jamaica Inn (93.50) A 1950 colonial manor long favored by Britain's upper crust. Balcony suites now have marble bathrooms. Ocho Rios; 800/837-4608 or 876/974-2514; jamaicainn.com; doubles from $$$.

Ritz-Carlton Rose Hall (86.84) Über-opulent mansion set on 5,000 acres with plenty of activities (there's golf, a spa, shopping, and more). Montego Bay; 800/241-3333 or 876/953-2800; ritzcarlton.com; doubles from $$.

Round Hill Hotel & Villas (87.33) A 119-room hideaway; legendary guests include John F. Kennedy and Liz Taylor. Montego Bay; 800/972-2159 or 876/956-7050; roundhilljamaica.com; doubles from $$$.

Sandals Whitehouse European Village & Spa (88.50) Three Euro-style villages (Italian, French, and Dutch) on a beach. Westmoreland; 800/726-3257 or 876/640-3000; sandals.com; doubles from $$$$$, including meals.

NEVIS
Nisbet Plantation Beach Club
(95.75) An 18th-century great house and 15 yellow cottages; the Caribbean's only historic plantation inn set on the beach. 800/742-6008 or 869/469-9325; nisbetplantation.com; doubles from $$$.

ST. BART'S
Eden Rock (87.57) This 34-room hotel on a rocky promontory is a Hollywood favorite. Baie de St. Jean; 877/563-7105 or 590-590/297-9999; edenrockhotel.com; doubles from $$$$, including breakfast.

Hôtel Guanahani & Spa (88.71) Creole manse and the island's only stand-alone spa, fresh off a $6 million face-lift. Grand Cul de Sac; 800/216-3774 or 590-590/276-660; leguanahani.com; doubles from $$$$$, including breakfast.

Hôtel Le Toiny (89.18) On the Côte Sauvage, 15 bungalows, each with a plunge pool and a Jacuzzi tub. Anse de Toiny; 590-590/278-888; letoiny.com; doubles from $$$$$, including breakfast.

Hôtel Saint-Barth Isle de France (88.60) Beach club–style boutique hotel on the island's widest beach. Baie de Flamands; 800/810-4691 or 590-590/27-61-81; isle-de-france.com; doubles from $$$$, including breakfast.

ST. LUCIA

Anse Chastanet Resort *(88.00)* Hillside cottages set in a 600-acre forest on the island's volcanic southwestern coast. Soufrière; 800/223-1108; ansechastanet.com; doubles from $$.

Jade Mountain *(94.91)* The 28 open-air suites have either infinity pools or private Jacuzzis. Soufrière; 800/223-1108 or 758/459-7000; jademountain stlucia.com; doubles from $$$$$.

Ladera *(88.00)* On a former cocoa plantation; its 32 mountainside villas and suites are open to the elements. Soufrière; 866/290-0978 or 758/459-6600; ladera.com; doubles from $$$, including breakfast.

Sandals Regency La Toc Golf Resort & Spa *(87.33)* A 331-room mega-resort (seven restaurants; the island's largest swimming pool). Castries; 800/726-3257 or 758/452-3081; sandals.com; doubles from $$$$$, all-inclusive.

TURKS & CAICOS

Grace Bay Club *(86.40)* Resort complex with an adults-only wing, family villas, and a new 5,157-square-foot gym and spa. Providenciales; 800/946-5757 or 649/946-5050; gracebayresorts.com; doubles from $$$$$, including breakfast.

Parrot Cay *(87.40)* Feng shui–approved Asian accents along a mile of shoreline. Providenciales; 877/754-0726 or 649/946-7788; parrotcay.como.bz; doubles from $$$$, including breakfast.

Regent Palms *(89.19)* These 72 suites have all the makings of a residence (in-room washer/dryers; full kitchens). Grace Bay Beach; 866/877-7256 or 649/946-8666; regentturksandcaicos.com; doubles from $$$$, including breakfast.

Mexico & Central & South America

ARGENTINA
BARILOCHE

Llao Llao Hotel & Resort, Golf-Spa *(87.68)* A 1940 lakeside lodge in the snowcapped Andes. 800/223-6800 or 54-29/4444-8530; llaollao.com; doubles from $$.

BUENOS AIRES

Alvear Palace Hotel *(92.25)* French-inspired 1932 building in stylish Recoleta. 1891 Avda. Alvear; 877/457-6315 or 54-11/4808-2100; alvearpalace.com; doubles from $$, including breakfast.

Four Seasons Hotel *(91.00)* A 1916 mansion and contemporary 13-story tower, connected by French-style gardens. 1086-1088 Calle Posadas; 800/332-3442 or 54 11/4321 1200; fourseasons.com; doubles from $$.

Hilton *(86.44)* Business hotel with a heated rooftop pool, in Puerto Madero. 351 Macacha Guemes; 800/445-8667 or 54-11/4891-0000; hilton.com; doubles from $.

Palacio Duhau - Park Hyatt *(92.00)* State-of-the-art hotel composed of a Belle Époque mansion and a 17-story addition, plus a 700-label wine cellar. 1661 Avda. Alvear; 800/223-1234 or 54-11/5171-1234; park.hyatt.com; doubles from $$$.

Park Tower, a Luxury Collection Hotel *(86.22)* Every guest gets a butler at this downtown mainstay with outdoor tennis courts. 1193 Avda. Alem; 800/325-3589 or 54-11/4318-9100; luxurycollection.com; doubles from $$, including breakfast.

Sofitel Arroyo *(87.81)* Landmark Neoclassical high-rise (the city's first skyscraper). The Art Deco interiors were designed by Pierre-Yves

Lounging porch-side at one of the villas at the Turtle Inn, in Placencia, Belize.

Rochon. 841 Calle Arroyo; 800/763-4835 or 54-11/4131-0125; sofitel.com; doubles from $$$.

BELIZE
PLACENCIA

Turtle Inn *(86.29)* Director Francis Ford Coppola's Balinese-inspired cottages on the country's only white-sand beach. 800/746-3743 or 011-501/824-4912; coppolaresorts.com; doubles from $$, including breakfast.

SAN IGNACIO

Blancaneaux Lodge *(92.73)* Another Coppola-owned property: 20 cabanas set amid jungle waterfalls near the Mayan ruins of Caracol. 800/746-3743 or 011-501/

824-4912; coppolaresorts.com; doubles from $$, including breakfast.

CHILE
SANTIAGO

Ritz-Carlton *(91.65)* In the chic El Golf neighborhood, 205 rooms; three new restaurants will open in 2011. 15 Calle El Alcalde; 800/241-3333 or 56-2/470-8500; ritzcarlton.com; doubles from $$, including breakfast.

COSTA RICA
GUANACASTE

Four Seasons Resort Costa Rica at Peninsula Papagayo *(88.44)* A resort with all the trimmings on a tranquil peninsula in a tropical dry

KEY

$ = UNDER $250
$$ = $250–$499
$$$ = $500–$749
$$$$ = $750–$999
$$$$$ = $1,000 & UP

forest. 800/332-3442 or 506/2696-0000; fourseasons.com; doubles from $$$.

ECUADOR
QUITO
JW Marriott Hotel (88.35) Pyramid-shaped hotel with the city's largest heated pool, in the financial and entertainment district. 1172 Avda. Orellana; 800/228-9290 or 593-2/297-2000; jwmarriott.com; doubles from $.

GUATEMALA
ANTIGUA
Hotel Museo Casa Santo Domingo (90.00) A 16th-century convent turned hotel and colonial-art museum, set in a UNESCO World Heritage site surrounded by volcanoes. 502/7820-1222; casasantodomingo.com.gt; doubles from $$.

MEXICO
ACAPULCO
Las Brisas (89.28) On Acapulco Bay, 251 pink-and-white casitas with plunge pools and 40 acres of hibiscus gardens. 5255 Crta. Escénica; 866/427-2779 or 52-744/469-6900; brisashotelonline.com; doubles from $$, including breakfast.

CANCÚN
CasaMagna Marriott Resort (87.83) Family-friendly hacienda with nine restaurants. Km 14.5, Blvd. Kukulcán; 800/228-9290 or 52-998/881-2000; casamagnacancun.com; doubles from $.

Fiesta Americana Grand Coral Beach Resort & Spa (87.20) Mammoth resort that welcomes an international crowd. Km 9.5, Blvd.

Kukulcán; 800/223-6800 or 52-998/881-3200; fiestamericanagrand.com; doubles from $$.

Hilton Cancún Golf & Spa Resort (87.04) A 426-room resort with seven infinity pools, close to the airport. Km 17, Blvd. Kukulcán; 800/445-8667 or 52-998/881-8000; hilton.com; doubles from $.

Le Méridien Resort & Spa (87.56) The European-style spa is the draw at this eight-story boutique resort. 37-1 Retorno del Rey; 888/624-5144 or 52-998/881-2200; lemeridien.com; doubles from $.

Ritz-Carlton (89.84) A 365-room retreat with tequila tastings and salsa lessons. 36 Retorno del Rey; 800/241-3333 or 52-998/881-0808; ritzcarlton.com; doubles from $$.

LOS CABOS
Esperanza, an Auberge Resort (92.91) 57 rooms and an infinity pool overlooking a private cove. Punta Ballena; 866/311-2226 or 52-624/145-6400; esperanzaresort.com; doubles from $$$, including breakfast.

Las Ventanas al Paraíso, A Rosewood Resort (90.40) A 71-suite hideaway known for superb service, with views of the Sea of Cortés. San José del Cabo; 888/767-3966 or 52-624/144-2800; lasventanas.com; doubles from $$$$.

Meliá Cabo Real All-Inclusive Beach & Golf Resort (87.29) Family-friendly hotel on a white-sand beach. San José del Cabo; 866/436-3542 or 52-624/144-2222; meliacaboreal.com; doubles from $$, all-inclusive.

One&Only Palmilla (92.69) Large resort with a boutique sensibility (butler service; personalized mini-bars) and great food. San José del

Cabo; 866/552-0001 or 52-624/146-7000; oneandonlyresorts.com; doubles from $$$.

Pueblo Bonito Pacifica Resort & Spa (89.52) New adults-only oasis that's illuminated by fire pits come evening. Cabo San Lucas; 800/990-8250 or 52-624/142-9696; pueblo bonitopacifica.com; doubles from $$.

MEXICO CITY
Four Seasons Hotel (95.00) A colonial-style hacienda with the city's largest rooms and a fleet of chauffeured vehicles on a historic promenade. 500 Paseo de la Reforma; 800/332-3442 or 52-55/5230-1818; fourseasons.com; doubles from $$.

JW Marriott Hotel (89.14) A 26-story business hotel in the Polanco district. The outdoor pool deck overlooks Chapultepec Park. 29 Calle Andrés Bello; 800/228-9290 or 52-55/5999-0000; jwmarriott.com; doubles from $$.

PUNTA MITA
Four Seasons Resort (90.92) On an isthmus near Puerto Vallarta, 173 rooms, plus a new Asian-inspired restaurant and Jack Nicklaus–designed golf course. 800/332-3442 or 52-329/291-6000; fourseasons.com; doubles from $$$.

RIVIERA MAYA
Fairmont Mayakoba (87.20) Guests at the Riviera Maya's first eco-resort look out on 50 acres of white-sand beach, freshwater lagoons, and canals. Solidaridad; 800/441-1414 or 52-984/206-3000; fairmont.com; doubles from $$$$.

PERU
CUZCO
Hotel Monasterio (90.88) A 16th-century monastery with Cuzquenian art and Baroque

interiors. 136 Calle Palacio, Plazoleta Nazarenas; 800/237-1236 or 51-84/604-000; monasteriohotel.com; doubles from $$$, including breakfast.

LIMA
JW Marriott Hotel (89.09) A 25-story glass tower just steps from the cliffs of Miraflores and popular shopping district Lacomar. 615 Malecón de la Reserva; 800/228-9290 or 51-1/217-7000; jwmarriott.com; doubles from $$.

MACHU PICCHU
Inkaterra Machu Picchu Pueblo Hotel (90.69) Terra-cotta-roofed casitas and plunge pools in the cloud forest below Machu Picchu. 800/442-5042; inkaterra.com; doubles from $$, including breakfast and dinner.

Machu Picchu Sanctuary Lodge (88.21) A 31-room stone luxury lodge—the only hotel next to the 15th-century Incan site. 800/237-1236; sanctuarylodgehotel.com; doubles from $1,025, all-inclusive.

URUGUAY
CARMELO
Four Seasons Resort (91.53) Nestled among pine and eucalyptus trees, with golf and an Asian-influenced spa. Km 262, Ruta 21; 800/332-3442 or 598-4542/9000; fourseasons.com; doubles from $$.

Europe
AUSTRIA
SALZBURG
Hotel Goldener Hirsch, a Luxury Collection Hotel (88.08) Near Mozart's former residence, an atmospheric 70-room property dating to the 15th century. 37 Getreidegasse; 800/325-3589 or 43-662/80840; goldenerhirschsalzburg.com; doubles from $$$$.

Hotel Sacher Salzburg *(89.82)*
Grand 1866 hotel on the Salzach
River. Oversize windows look
out onto postcard-worthy views of
Old Town. 5-7 Schwarzstrasse;
800/223-6800 or 43-662/889-770;
sacher.com; doubles from $$$.

VIENNA
**Hotel Imperial, a Luxury
Collection Hotel** *(91.52)* An 1863
palace on the Ring with traditional
interiors and a stellar concierge staff.
16 Kärntner Ring; 800/325-3589 or
43-1/501-100; hotelimperialvienna.
com; doubles from $$$.

Hotel Sacher Wien *(90.17)*
Belle Époque property opposite
the opera house; Pierre-Yves Rochon
has refurbished the rooms.
4 Philharmonikerstrasse; 800/223-
6800 or 43-662/889-770; sacher.
com; doubles from $$$.

BELGIUM
BRUSSELS
Hotel Amigo *(86.95)* Once a
16th-century brick prison near
the Grand Place; now a light-filled
hotel with surrealist art. Rue de
l'Amigo; 888/667-9477 or 32-2/
547-4747; hotelamigo.com; doubles
from $$.

CZECH REPUBLIC
PRAGUE
Four Seasons Hotel *(90.33)* Four
architecturally distinct buildings on
the east bank of the Vltava River.
Renovations will be completed in
June 2011. 2A/1098 Veleslavinova;
800/332-3442 or 420-221/427-777;
fourseasons.com; doubles from $$$.

Mandarin Oriental *(92.94)* In the
heart of the historic Malá Strana
district, a restored 14th-century
monastery, plus a modern wing.
459/1 Nebovidská; 800/526-6566 or
420-2/3308-8888; mandarinoriental.
com; doubles from $$.

ENGLAND
BATH
Royal Crescent Hotel *(90.90)* Two
18th-century row houses and a
holistic spa at the center of Bath's
semicircle of Georgian-era
residences. 16 Royal Crescent;
800/735-2478 or 44-1225/823-333;
royalcrescent.co.uk; doubles from
$$$, including breakfast.

LONDON
Brown's Hotel *(90.43)* Eleven
Georgian town houses in Mayfair
combine history (Churchill and
Kipling were guests) with
contemporary interiors. Albemarle
St.; 888/667-9477 or 44-20/7493-
6020; roccofortecollection.com;
doubles from $$$.

Claridge's *(89.79)* Landmark
property, steps from Bond Street
boutiques, with Art Deco elements
and Gordon Ramsay restaurant
Diane von Furstenberg designed 20
rooms and suites. Brook St.;
866/599-6991 or 44-20/7629-8860;
claridges.co.uk; doubles from $$.

The Connaught *(88.00)* A red-brick
Victorian classic in Mayfair with
123 expertly-restored rooms and a
stylish bar by designer David Collins.
Carlos Place; 866/599-6991 or 44-
20/7499-7070; the-connaught.co.uk;
doubles from $$$.

Covent Garden Hotel *(86.55)* In
the heart of the theater district, 58
rooms with an eclectic mix of
traditional English furniture and
modern art. 10 Monmouth St.;
800/553-6674 or 44-20/7806-1000;
firmdale.com; doubles from $$.

Dukes Hotel *(87.39)* Discreet 90-
room hotel on a quiet cul-de-sac
steps from Green Park and St.
James's Palace. St. James's Place;
800/381-4702 or 44-20/7491-4840;
dukeshotel.com; doubles from $$$.

The Royal staircase in
Vienna's Hotel Imperial.

Four Seasons Hotel *(86.76)* An
11-story tower near Hyde Park
Corner, newly reopened after a two-
year, head-to-toe renovation by
Pierre-Yves Rochon. Hamilton Place;
800/332-3442 or 44-20/7499-0888;
fourseasons.com; doubles from $$$.

The Goring *(91.06)* A family-owned
hotel near Buckingham Palace that
layers charming touches with the best
of British design (Nina Campbell; Tim
Gosling; Russell Sage). Beeston Place;
800/987-7433 or 44-20/7396-9000;
thegoring.com; doubles from $$$.

**The Lanesborough, a St. Regis
Hotel** *(93.47)* Elegant Georgian
building on Hyde Park Corner with

95 rooms. The Library Bar stocks
hard-to-find whiskeys; the Garden
Room has a new walk-in humidor.
Hyde Park Corner; 877/787-3447 or
44-20/7259-5599; lanesborough.
com; doubles from $$$$.

Mandarin Oriental Hyde Park
(87.39) This former Victorian
gentleman's club across from
Harvey Nichols has new restaurants
from Daniel Boulud and Heston
Blumenthal. 66 Knightsbridge;
800/526-6566 or 44-20/7235-2000;
mandarinoriental.com; doubles
from $$$$.

The Milestone *(89.47)* The 62
rooms of this hotel, opposite

Kensington Palace, are individually decorated to imbue the property with a residential feel. 1 Kensington Court; 800/223-6800 or 44-20/7917-1000; milestonehotel.com; doubles from $$.

The Savoy (87.41) Legendary Edwardian and Art Deco Thames-front property, recently reopened after a three-year, $350 million restoration, said to be the biggest in British history. The Strand; 800/441-1414 or 44-20/7836-4343; the-savoy. com; doubles from $$$.

The Stafford (93.44) Refined town house (currently undergoing a renovation) behind Green Park with an extraordinary wine cellar and a world-class restaurant opening this summer. St. James's Place; 800/426-3135 or 44-20/7493-0111; thestaffordhotel.co.uk; doubles from $$.

FRANCE
BURGUNDY
Hôtel Le Cep (88.75) Cluster of small 14th- to 18th-century mansions housing 64 antiques-filled rooms in the heart of wine country. Beaune; 800/542-4800 or 33-3/80-22-35-48; hotel-cep-beaune.com; doubles from $.

CANNES
InterContinental Carlton (86.63) A 1911 palace with nine refurbished suites on the seventh floor. 58 Blvd. de la Croisette; 800/327-0200 or 33-4/93-06-40-06; intercontinental. com; doubles from $$$$, including breakfast.

CARCASSONNE
Hôtel de la Cité (90.48) A stately 1909 hotel with stained-glass windows—plus a new terrace bar for cocktails and small plates. 800/237-1236; hoteldelacite.com; doubles from $$$.

CÔTE D'AZUR
Château de la Chèvre d'Or (92.71) Stone buildings and a Michelin two-starred restaurant set on a cliff above the Mediterranean. Èze Village; 800/735-2478 or 33-4/92-10-66-66; chevredor.com; doubles from $$.

Hôtel Château Eza (93.33) Secluded 17th-century hotel built into the ancient rock walls of a medieval village. Èze Village; 33-4/93-41-12-24; chateaueza.com; doubles from $$$.

LOIRE VALLEY
Domaine des Hauts de Loire (95.00) Former hunting lodge with 32 rooms (some Empire-style) on 178 forested acres between Blois and Amboise. Onzain; 800/735-2478 or 33-2/54-20-72-57; domainehautsloire. com; doubles from $.

PARIS
Four Seasons Hotel George V (92.76) A 1928 icon near the Champs-Élysées, with commanding views of Paris, and an award-winning spa. 31 Ave. George V; 800/332-3442 or 33-1/49-52-70-00; fourseasons.com; doubles from $$$$$.

Hôtel de Crillon (94.40) Louis XV–commissioned palace; there's a new head chef at recently reopened Les Ambassadeurs restaurant. 10 Place de la Concorde; 800/223-6800 or 33-1/44-71-15-00; crillon.com; doubles from $$$$$.

Hôtel Le Bristol (88.16) Grand property known for 320-square-foot standard rooms—the city's largest. 112 Rue du Faubourg St.-Honoré; 800/745-8883 or 33-1/53-43-43-00; lebristolparis.com; doubles from $$$$$.

Hôtel Le Meurice (90.04) Regal Dorchester Collection hotel with Louis XVI–style interiors and public spaces by Philippe Starck. The 205 rooms and suites were redesigned by Charles Jouffre. 228 Rue de Rivoli; 800/650-1842 or 33-1/44-58-10-10; lemeurice.com; doubles from $$$$.

Hôtel Plaza Athénée (89.60) A Haussmann-era Dorchester Collection hotel with a Michelin three-starred restaurant and Eiffel Tower views. 25 Ave. Montaigne; 800/650-1842 or 33-1/53-67-66-65; plaza-athenee-paris.com; doubles from $$$$$.

Park Hyatt Paris-Vendôme (91.33) Palace-style hotel defined by sleek interiors—a departure from its more traditional neighbors—just off Place Vendôme. 5 Rue de la Paix; 877/875-4658 or 33-1/58-71-12-34; park.hyatt. com; doubles from $$$$$.

Ritz Paris (89.94) A 159-room manse (filled with gilded touches) built by César Ritz in 1898 and the home of Coco Chanel for 37 years. 15 Place Vendôme; 800/223-6800 or 33-1/43-16-30-30; ritzparis.com; doubles from $$$$$.

The 19th-century former hunting lodge at Domaine des Hauts de Loire, in France's Loire Valley.

PROVENCE

La Colombe d'Or *(91.67)* In the 1920's, an inn where artists gathered; now a charming hotel with 25 rooms filled with paintings by luminaries including Klee and Calder. 1 Place du Général de Gaulle, St.-Paul de Vence; 33-4/93-32-80-02; la-colombe-dor. com; doubles from $$.

L'Oustau de Baumanière *(89.14)* Provençal property near Arles with three farmhouses, two pools, and a renowned restaurant. Les-Baux-de-Provence; 800/735-2478 or 33-4/90-54-33-07; oustaudebaumaniere.com; doubles from $$.

Villa Gallici *(87.05)* Lavish 19th-century villa surrounded by Florentine gardens; the 22 rooms are furnished with canopy beds and chinoiscric wallpaper. Ave. de la Violette, Aix-en-Provence; 33-4/42-23-29-23; villagallici.com; doubles from $$$.

REIMS

Les Crayères *(91.09)* Impeccable turn-of-the-20th-century château in the heart of the Champagne region. 64 Blvd. Henry Vasnier; 800/735-2478 or 33-3/26-24-90-00; lescrayeres.com; doubles from $$$.

GERMANY
ROTHENBURG OB DER TAUBER

Hotel Eisenhut *(89.56)* Series of 15th- and 16th-century mansions in the Bavarian town's medieval walled center. 49-98/617-050; arvena.de; doubles from $.

GREECE
ATHENS

Hotel Grande Bretagne, a Luxury Collection Hotel *(89.97)* An 1874 property opposite Parliament with antiques and white-gloved valets. Constitution Square; 800/325-3589 or 30-210/333-0000; grandebretagne.gr; doubles from $$$$.

King George Palace *(86.85)* Glitzy Neoclassical hotel just off Constitution Square; the 102 rooms feature raw-silk bedspreads and Murano chandeliers. 3 Vas. Georgiou A' Str.; 800/223-6800 or 30-210/322-2210; classicalhotels. com; doubles from $$, including breakfast.

SANTORINI

Katikies Hotel *(89.33)* Newly renovated white-on-white property seemingly sculpted into the cliffs above the Aegean. Oia; 800/223-6800; katikieshotelssantorini.com; doubles from $$$.

HUNGARY
BUDAPEST

Four Seasons Hotel Gresham Palace *(92.96)* Art Nouveau masterpiece at the base of the Chain Bridge. 5-6 Roosevelt Tér; 800/332-3442 or 36 1/268 6000; fourseasons. com; doubles from $$.

InterContinental *(87.05)* A 402-room hotel and spa with views of the Danube to Castle Hill. 12-14 Apáczai Csere János Utca; 800/327-0200 or 36-1/327-6333; intercontinental.com; doubles from $.

IRELAND
COUNTY CLARE

Dromoland Castle *(90.62)* A 16th-century estate along Lough Dromoland, 15 minutes north of Shannon Airport. Newmarket-on-Fergus; 800/346-7007 or 353-61/368-144; dromoland.ie; doubles from $$.

COUNTY KERRY

Sheen Falls Lodge *(91.47)* Waterside property with classic country interiors on 300 acres off the Ring of Kerry. Kenmare; 800/735-2478 or 353-64/66-41600; sheenfallslodge.ie; doubles from $$.

COUNTY KILKENNY

Mount Juliet *(87.53)* Irish sporting estate that offers a full roster of activities, including golf and horseback riding. Thomastown; 800/525-4800 or 353-56/777-3000; mountjuliet.ie; doubles from $$.

COUNTY LIMERICK

Adare Manor Hotel & Golf Resort *(87.78)* An 1832 Gothic Revival castle set among parterre gardens and a Robert Trent Jones Sr.–designed golf course. Adare; 800/223-6800 or 353-61/396-566; adaremanor.com; doubles from $$$.

COUNTY MAYO

Ashford Castle *(90.63)* A sprawling 1228 crenellated estate on 350 acres along the banks of the salmon- and trout-filled Lough Corrib. 800/223-6800; ashford.ie; doubles from $$, including breakfast.

DUBLIN

Four Seasons Hotel *(93.68)* New-build hotel done up in British country style in an affluent suburb. Simmonscourt Rd.; 800/332-3442 or 353-1/665-4000; fourseasons.com; doubles from $.

The Merrion *(90.67)* Four Georgian houses overlooking formal gardens near the National Gallery; the hotel's art collection includes works by 20th-century Irish painters. Upper Merrion St.; 800/223-6800 or 353-1/603-0600; merrionhotel.com; doubles from $$$$.

The Shelbourne *(89.03)* Historic Georgian building—Ireland's first constitution was drafted here in 1922—facing St. Stephen's Green. 27 St. Stephen's Green; 800/228-9290 or 353-1/663-4500; renaissancehotels.com; doubles from $$.

ITALY
AMALFI COAST

Grand Hotel Excelsior Vittoria *(88.67)* Three adjoining brick buildings above the Bay of Naples, owned and operated by the same family since 1834. Sorrento; 800/325-8541 or 39-08/1877-7111; excelsiorvittoria.com; doubles from $$$, including breakfast.

Hotel Santa Caterina *(90.72)* A 94-room seaside villa owned by the same family since 1880. An infinity pool will be added this year. Amalfi; 800/223-6800 or 39-08/987-1012; hotelsantacaterina.it; doubles from $$$, including breakfast.

Il San Pietro *(90.71)* Cliff-hanging architectural wonder, set high above the Amalfi Coast, with 84 rooms and a private beach reachable via elevator. Positano; 800/735-2478 or 39-08/987-5455; ilsanpietro.it; doubles from $$$, including breakfast.

Le Sirenuse *(94.88)* A dignified 61-room hotel (the former 1951 summer residence of the Marchesi Sersale); four junior suites are on the horizon. Positano; 800/223-6800 or 39-08/987-5066; sirenuse.it; doubles from $$$, including breakfast.

Palazzo Sasso *(95.17)* A 12th-century aristocratic Italian palazzo with 43 rooms and a Michelin-starred restaurant. Ravello; 800/323-7500 or 39-08/981-8181; palazzosasso.com; doubles from $$, including breakfast.

ASOLO

Hotel Villa Cipriani *(90.11)* Once the home of Robert Browning, set in a garden of pomegranate trees

above the town. 39-04/2352-3411; villaciprianiasolo.com; doubles from $, including breakfast.

BOLOGNA
Grand Hotel Majestic Già Baglioni (86.75) An 18th-century property near the cathedral of Bologna. A wellness center opens in 2011. 8 Via Indipendenza; 800/223-6800 or 39-05/122-5445; duetorrihotels.com; doubles from $$$, including breakfast.

CAPRI
Grand Hotel Quisisana (89.93) A luxurious 148-room hotel and spa (with Capri's only hammam) near Piazza Umberto. 800/223-6800 or 39-08/1837-0788; quisisana.com; doubles from $$, including breakfast.

CORTONA
Il Falconiere (88.75) Classic 17th-century Tuscan villa-estate outside Arezzo, with 22 rooms and a 25-acre vineyard. 800/735-2478 or 39-05/7561-2679; ilfalconiere.it; doubles from $$, including breakfast.

FLORENCE
Four Seasons Hotel Firenze (91.27) A 1472 resort-style palace near the Duomo, with 160 impeccable rooms, next to a centuries-old private park. 99 Borgo Pinti; 800/332-3442 or 39-05/526261; fourseasons.com; doubles from $$$.

Grand Hotel Villa Medici (87.86) An 18th-century hotel near the Uffizi, with exquisite details and the only outdoor pool in Florence. 42 Via Il Prato; 800/223-6800 or 39-05/527-7171; villamedicihotel.com; doubles from $$$.

Hotel Helvetia & Bristol (86.44) A 67-room palazzo featuring 17th-century paintings and antiques, set in front of the 1489 Palazzo Strozzi palace. 2 Via Dei Pescioni; 39-055/26651; royaldemeure.com; doubles from $$$.

Hotel Lungarno (86.36) Handsome 73-room medieval building filled with modern art—Picasso and Cocteau—near the Ponte Vecchio on the Arno. 14 Borgo San Jacopo; 39-055/27261; lungarnohotels.com; doubles from $$$.

Westin Excelsior (88.66) A 300-label wine cellar and a new rooftop restaurant, plus 171 rooms, in a 15th-century palace near the Ponte Vecchio. 3 Piazza Ognissanti; 800/228-3000 or 39-05/527-151; westin.com; doubles from $$$.

FLORENCE AREA
Hotel Villa San Michele (91.80) Lemon-scented gardens and a façade attributed to Michelangelo at a 15th-century hilltop villa. Fiesole; 800/237-1236 or 39-05/5567-8200; villasanmichele.com; doubles from $$$$$, including breakfast.

LAKE COMO
Grand Hotel Villa Serbelloni (87.91) Aristocratic 19th-century villa flanked by woodlands, on a promontory that stretches out to the center of Lake Como. Bellagio; 800/860-8672 or 39-03/195-0216; villaserbelloni.com; doubles from $$$, including breakfast.

Villa d'Este (93.66) Regal 1568 lakefront estate built as a private residence for a cardinal, set within 25 acres of parkland along Lake Como. Cernobbio; 800/223-6800 or 39-03/13481; villadeste.it; doubles from $$$$, including breakfast.

MILAN
Four Seasons Hotel (91.77) A dramatic 118-room hotel in a 15th-century convent, steps from Milan's best shopping; a new spa opens in 2011. 6/8 Via Gesù; 800/332-3442 or 39-02/77088; fourseasons.com; doubles from $$$$.

Hotel Principe di Savoia (88.55) Part of the Dorchester Collection, this Neoclassical building—a gathering place since the 1920's—has modern amenities (and a full-service gym, too). 17 Piazza della Repubblica; 800/650-1842 or 39-02/62301; hotelprincipedisavoia.com; doubles from $$$$$.

PORTOFINO
Hotel Splendido (93.52) A flower-filled hillside villa (a monastery in the 14th and 15th centuries) that overlooks the bay. 800/223-6800; hotelsplendido.com; doubles from $$$$$, including breakfast.

ROME
Hotel de Russie (90.59) Stylish 1814 palazzo located on the fashionable Via del Babuino, best-known for its terraced gardens. 9 Via del Babuino; 888/667-9477 or 39-06/328-881; roccofortecollection.com; doubles from $$$$.

Hotel Hassler Roma (90.94) Turn-of-the-century palace hotel at the top of the Spanish Steps. Its Il Vicolletto wing was just renovated. 6 Piazza Trinità dei Monti; 888/787-3447 or 39-06/699-340; hotelhasslerroma.com; doubles from $$$$.

Regina Hotel Baglioni (89.87) Belle Époque property with Art Deco furnishings in all 135 rooms, minutes from the Spanish Steps. 72 Via Veneto; 39-06/421-111; baglionihotels.com; doubles from $$$$.

St. Regis Grand Hotel (86.93) Beds come with tufted headboards, and bathrooms are done in travertine marble at this 184-room retreat near the Trevi Fountain. 3 Via Vittorio E. Orlando; 877/787-3447 or 39-06/47091; stregis.com; doubles from $$$.

TAORMINA
Grand Hotel Timeo (90.22) A 19th-century residence inherited from Sicilian nobility—the first hotel to be built here—overlooking Mount Etna. The 72 Baroque rooms will be refurbished by new owner Orient-Express in 2011. 800/237-1236 or 39-09/4262-70200; grandhoteltimeo.com; doubles from $$$.

VENICE
Bauer Hotel (88.22) Sustainability (solar-powered boat; all-natural amenities) is the focus at this sister hotel to Bauer Il Palazzo. San Marco 1459; 800/223-6800 or 39-04/1520-7022; bauervenezia.com; doubles from $$$, including breakfast.

Bauer Il Palazzo (86.44) 82-room palazzo turned boutique hotel in the heart of Venice, with its own Grand Canal berth. San Marco 1413/d; 800/223-6800 or 39-04/1520-7022; ilpalazzovenezia.com; doubles from $$$, including breakfast

Hotel Cipriani (87.30) Two historic palazzos and a 1950's-era main building, on Giudecca Island. The hotel also has an arcade and couture boutiques. Giudecca 10; 800/237-1236 or 39-04/1520-7744; hotelcipriani.com; doubles from $$$$$, including breakfast.

Hotel Danieli, a Luxury Collection Hotel (86.95) Three palaces from the 14th, 19th, and 20th centuries, with 225 rooms overlooking the Venice lagoon. 4196 Riva degli Schiavoni; 800/325-3589; danielihotelvenice.com; doubles from $$$$$.

Hotel Gritti Palace, a Luxury Collection Hotel *(89.94)* An old-world atmosphere in a 16th-century Renaissance palace on the banks of the Grand Canal. 2467 Campo Santa Maria del Giglio; 800/325-3589; hotelgrittipalacevenice.com; doubles from $$$$$.

Hotel Monaco & Grand Canal *(88.00)* 17th-century pedigreed palazzo at the mouth of the Grand Canal, with sweeping views of San Giorgio Island. San Marco 1332; 800/457-4000 or 39-04/1520-0211; hotelmonaco.it; doubles from $$$$, including breakfast.

Luna Hotel Baglioni *(89.00)* A 900-year-old aristocratic palazzo—the oldest in Venice—steps from the famed Piazza San Marco. San Marco 1243; 800/223-6800 or 39-04/1528-9840; baglionihotels.com; doubles from $$$$$.

Westin Europa & Regina *(88.31)* Five 18th- and 19th-century Venetian palaces on the Grand Canal, with unsurpassed views of Santa Maria della Salute, the city's iconic 17th-century church. San Marco 2159; 800/228-3000 or 39-04/1240-0001; westin.com; doubles from $$$$$.

MONACO
MONTE CARLO
Hôtel de Paris Monte-Carlo *(90.91)* Marble-and-gilt Belle Époque structure on the Place du Casino, home to Alain Ducasse's Louis XV restaurant. Place du Casino; 800/223-6800; en.hoteldeparismontecarlo.com; doubles from $$$$.

NETHERLANDS
AMSTERDAM
Hotel Pulitzer, a Luxury Collection Hotel *(86.88)* The 25 interconnected canal houses

date from the 17th and 18th centuries. 315-331 Prinsengracht; 800/325-3589 or 31-20/523-5235; pulitzeramsterdam.com; doubles from $$$.

POLAND
WARSAW
Le Méridien Bristol *(87.47)* Fin-de-siècle property near Old Town on Warsaw's architecture-rich Royal Route. 42-44 Krakowskie Przedmiescie; 800/543-3000 or 48-22/551-1000; lemeridien.com; doubles from $$.

PORTUGAL
LISBON
Olissippo Lapa Palace *(94.60)* Hilltop hotel surrounded by gardens in the embassy district, built in 1870 as a private villa. 4 Rua do Pau de Bandeira; 800/237-1236 or 351/213-949-494; lapapalace.com; doubles from $$.

SCOTLAND
EDINBURGH
The Balmoral *(90.25)* Edwardian hotel with a 195-foot clock tower and subtly modern interiors, located next to Waverly Station. 1 Princes St.; 888/667-9477; thebalmoralhotel.com; doubles from $$$.

ST. ANDREWS
Old Course Hotel, Golf Resort & Spa *(89.33)* Adjacent to the world's oldest course, this golf resort has touches both classic (striped wallpapers; velvet upholstery) and contemporary (23 suites designed by Jacques Garcia). 800/745-8883 or 44-1334/474-371; oldcoursehotel.co.uk; doubles from $$$.

SPAIN
BARCELONA
Hotel Arts *(89.66)* Ritz-Carlton–managed hotel in a 44-story tower rising above the seafront at Port Olimpic, with a buzzy pool scene. 19-21 Carr. de la Marina; 800/241-

A junior suite at the Grand Hôtel, in Stockholm.

3333 or 34-93/221-1000; ritzcarlton.com; doubles from $$$.

MADRID
Westin Palace *(87.28)* Grand 1912 hotel with a massive stained-glass dome, steps from the Prado and Thyssen museums. 7 Plaza de las Cortes; 800/228-3000; westin.com; doubles from $$$.

MARBELLA
Marbella Club Hotel *(87.06)* Discreet beachfront property with private villas on Marbella's Golden Mile. Blvd. Principe Alfonso Von Hohenlohe; 800/223-6800 or 34-95/282-2211; marbellaclub.com; doubles from $$$.

SAN SEBASTIÁN
Hotel Maria Cristina, a Luxury Collection Hotel *(87.00)* Belle Époque hotel known for its old-world style, two blocks from Old Town. 4 Paseo República Argentina; 800/325-3589 or 34/94-343-7600; luxurycollection.com; doubles from $.

SWEDEN
STOCKHOLM
Grand Hôtel *(88.61)* Site of the first Nobel Prize ceremony, opposite the Royal Palace. The hotel's Mathias Dahlgren dining room was awarded two Michelin stars in 2010. 8 Södra Blasieholmshamnen; 800/327-0200 or 46-8/679-3500; grandhotel.se; doubles from $$$$.

SWITZERLAND

INTERLAKEN

Victoria-Jungfrau Grand Hotel & Spa *(89.91)* A 212-room Alpine resort with Beaux-Arts interiors and an Asian-style spa. 800/223-6800 or 41-33/828-2828; victoria-jungfrau. ch; doubles from $$$$$.

ZURICH

Baur au Lac *(92.20)* Freshly renovated classic hotel—family-owned since 1844—with formal gardens overlooking Lake Zurich. 1 Talstrasse; 800/223-6800 or 41-44/220-5020; bauraulac.ch; doubles from $$$$.

Park Hyatt *(87.20)* Steps from Bahnhofstrasse boutiques in the financial district, a contemporary 2004 building. 21 Beethoven-Str.; 877/875-4658 or 41-43/883-1234; park. hyatt.com; doubles from $$.

TURKEY

ISTANBUL

Çirağan Palace Hotel Kempinski *(89.33)* Former sultan's palace with a modern annex on the Bosporus's European shore. 32 Çirağan Cadd.; 800/426-3135 or 90-212/326-4646; kempinski.com; doubles from $$$$.

Four Seasons Hotel Istanbul at Sultanahmet *(92.63)* Restored Neoclassical former prison in the Old City—around the corner from Hagia Sophia. 1 Tevkifhane Sk.; 800/332-3442 or 90-212/638-8200; fourseasons.com; doubles from $$$.

Ritz-Carlton *(86.74)* Ottoman-style luxury in a hilltop skyscraper near Taksim Square; rooms were refurbished in 2010. 9 Elmadag Sisli; 800/241-3333 or 90-212/334-4444; ritzcarlton.com; doubles from $$$.

Africa & the Middle East

BOTSWANA

CHOBE NATIONAL PARK

Sanctuary Chobe Chilwero *(86.53)* Adjacent to a national park that's home to Africa's largest elephant population, 15 cottages and Botswana's only full spa. 27-11/438-4650; sanctuaryretreats. com; doubles from $$$$$, all-inclusive.

MOREMI GAME RESERVE

Sanctuary Chief's Camp *(90.40)* Bush pavilions on an Okavango Delta island teeming with the Big Five. 27-11/438-4650; sanctuary retreats.com; doubles from $$$$$, all-inclusive.

EGYPT

ALEXANDRIA

Four Seasons Hotel at San Stefano *(90.25)* In a crescent-shaped building on the Corniche, 118 rooms with Neoclassical furniture and Roman-style baths. 399 El Geish Rd.; 800/332-3442; fourseasons.com; doubles from $$$.

CAIRO

Four Seasons Hotel at Nile Plaza *(89.95)* A 30-story high-rise with an award-winning spa and new Palace Suite by Pierre-Yves Rochon. 1089 Corniche El Nil; 800/332-3442; fourseasons.com; doubles from $$.

Four Seasons Hotel Cairo at the First Residence *(93.27)* A 269-room glass tower that blends the old and new, on the Nile opposite downtown Cairo. 35 Giza St.; 800/332-3442; fourseasons.com; doubles from $$.

JW Marriott *(86.44)* Resort-style property (golf course; water park) on 400 acres in upscale Heliopolis. Ring Rd.; 800/228-9290; marriott. com; doubles from $$.

Twelve Apostles Hotel's Azure restaurant, in Cape Town, South Africa.

Mena House Oberoi (86.87) 19th-century lodge with just-renovated modern wings on 40 acres abutting the Great Pyramid of Khufu. 6 Pyramids Rd.; 800/562-3764; oberoihotels.com; doubles from $$.

ISRAEL
JERUSALEM
King David Hotel (87.02) A swank 1930's property redone by Adam D. Tihany; close to Old City's Temple Mount and Western Wall. 23 King David St.; 800/223-7773; danhotels.com; doubles from $$.

JORDAN
AMMAN
Four Seasons Hotel (86.72) A 15-story stone-and-glass structure between Al Sweifyah residential area and the financial district. Fifth Circle, Al-Kindi St.; 800/332-3442; fourseasons.com; doubles from $$, including breakfast.

KENYA
AMBOSELI NATIONAL PARK
Tortilis Camp (94.12) The park's only luxe property, facing Mount Kilimanjaro. 254-20/603-090; chelipeacock.com; doubles from $$$$$, all-inclusive.

MASAI MARA
andBeyond Kichwa Tembo (93.71) Two camps managed by the safari outfitter andBeyond, recently lauded for its conservation efforts. 888/882-3742; andbeyondafrica.com; doubles from $$$$, all-inclusive.

Fairmont Mara Safari Club (96.31) 50 renovated tents on a Mara River oxbow (prime for hippo-viewing), plus balloon safaris. 800/441-1414; fairmont.com; doubles from $$$$$.

NAIROBI
Fairmont the Norfolk (86.76) Tudor-style hotel and tropical gardens—a frequent jumping-off point for safari travelers. Harry Thuku Rd.; 800/441-1414; fairmont.com; doubles from $$.

NANYUKI
Fairmont Mount Kenya Safari Club (92.29) Updated 1950's-era hunting lodge with croquet fields and stables. 800/441-1414; fairmont.com; doubles from $$$.

MOROCCO
FEZ
Sofitel Fès Palais Jamaï (86.56) Moorish- and Arabic-inspired 19th-century palace with 142 refurbished rooms and an authentic *caidale* tent. Bab Guissa; 800/763-4835; sofitel.com; doubles from $$.

MARRAKESH
La Mamounia (86.74) Legendary 1923 hotel, gleaming after a three-year, $180 million renovation by designer Jacques Garcia. Ave. Bab Jdid; 800/223-6800; mamounia.com; doubles from $$$.

SOUTH AFRICA
CAPE TOWN
Cape Grace (92.52) Refurbished hotel with 120 rooms, a spa, and a luxury yacht, on a private Victoria & Alfred Waterfront quay. W. Quay Rd.; 800/223-6800; capegrace.com; doubles from $$$.

Mount Nelson Hotel (87.64) A 209-room, pink stucco, 1899 property on nine green acres, convenient to beaches and Table Mountain. 76 Orange St.; 800/237-1236; mountnelson.co.za; doubles from $$, including breakfast.

Table Bay Hotel (87.17) Maritime-themed hotel featuring a 246-foot driveway lined with palm trees. Quay 6, Victoria & Alfred Waterfront; 27-21/406-5000; suninternational.com; doubles from $$$, including breakfast.

Twelve Apostles Hotel & Spa (93.62) Exclusive Cape Dutch–style hideaway, tucked between mountains and sea, with free shuttles to downtown, just 15 minutes away. Victoria Rd.; 800/223-6800; 12apostleshotel.com; doubles from $$$$$, including breakfast.

JOHANNESBURG
Michelangelo Hotel (87.11) Italian Renaissance–inspired hotel with grand public spaces and 242 refurbished suites on Nelson Mandela Square. 135 West St.; 800/223-6800; michelangelohotel.com; doubles from $$$, including breakfast.

Saxon Boutique Hotel, Villas & Spa (90.86) All-suite estate where Nelson Mandela was an extended guest in the 1990's; three new villas have added 29 rooms. 36 Saxon Rd.; 877/354-2213; saxon.co.za; doubles from $$$$$, including breakfast.

The Westcliff (89.22) Nine palatial, coral-pink structures on a ridge overlooking a cobblestoned courtyard and the city center. 67 Jan Smuts Ave.; 800/237-1236; westcliff.co.za; doubles from $$, including breakfast.

KRUGER NATIONAL PARK AREA
Londolozi Private Game Reserve (94.18) Five family-run camps (Pioneer was built this year) in an area known for leopard sightings. 800/735-2478; londolozi.com; doubles from $$$$$, all-inclusive.

MalaMala Game Reserve (93.07) Trio of renowned lodges (plus a wine cellar, library, and infinity pool) on South Africa's largest private Big Five preserve. 27-11/442-2267; malamala.com; doubles from $$$$$, all-inclusive.

Royal Malewane (94.67) A 20-room bush camp with throwback activities (rides in antique biplanes; horseback safaris). 27-15/793-0150; royalmalewane.com; doubles from $$$$$, all-inclusive.

Singita Kruger National Park (94.25) Two raised lodges with fashionable interiors by up-and-coming African designers. 800/735-2478; singita.com; doubles from $$$$$, all-inclusive.

Singita Sabi Sand (94.67) Pair of lodges—Boulders is high-design rustic, Ebony has a vintage safari feel—along the Sand River. 800/735-2478; singita.com; doubles from $$$$$, all-inclusive.

TANZANIA
NGORONGORO CRATER
Ngorongoro Crater Lodge (89.90) Masai-inspired huts with Victorian touches (Persian carpets; red roses) along a volcano rim. 888/882-3742; andbeyondafrica.com; doubles from $$$$$, all-inclusive.

Ngorongoro Sopa Lodge (88.55) Rondavels with floor-to-ceiling windows look down into a huge crater frequented by black rhinos. 800/806-9565; sopalodges.com; doubles from $$, including meals.

SERENGETI NATIONAL PARK
Serengeti Sopa Lodge (92.57) Secluded hotel with African interiors (driftwood furnishings; batik), set in an acacia grove overlooking the plains. 800/806-9565; sopalodges.com; doubles from $$, including meals.

UNITED ARAB EMIRATES
DUBAI

Burj Al Arab (*91.57*) Sail-shaped icon, on its own island off the Persian Gulf's Jumeirah Beach. The 202 suites are all serviced by butlers. Jumeirah Beach Rd.; 877/854-8051; jumeirah.com; doubles from $$$$$, including breakfast.

ZAMBIA
LIVINGSTONE

Royal Livingstone (*92.59*) 173 colonial rooms—all with private verandas and featuring wildlife sketches—next to Victoria Falls. 260-21/332-1122; suninternational. com; doubles from $$$$, including breakfast.

Asia
CAMBODIA
PHNOM PENH

Raffles Hotel Le Royal (*86.29*) 1920's French colonial–era mansion, updated with top-tier amenities. 92 Rukhak Vithei Daun Penh; 800/768-9009 or 855-23/981-888; raffles. com; doubles from $$.

SIEM REAP

Hôtel de la Paix (*93.75*) Cool and stylish 1950's hotel in the heart of Siem Reap. Sivutha Blvd.; 800/525-4800 or 855-63/966-000; hoteldelapaixangkor.com; doubles from $$.

Raffles Grand Hotel d'Angkor (*88.21*) Artfully restored grande dame with exacting service and a lap pool inspired by Angkor's royal baths. 1 Vithei Charles de Gaulle; 800/768-9009 or 855-63/963-888; raffles.com; doubles from $$.

CHINA
BEIJING

Grand Hotel (*86.62*) A 209-room Imperial-style hotel adjacent to the Forbidden City and Tiananmen Square. 35 E. Chang An Ave.; 800/223-6800 or 86-10/6513-7788; grandhotelbeijing.com; doubles from $$, including breakfast.

Grand Hyatt (*86.42*) Glittering, crescent-shaped building, a quick stroll from Tiananmen Square and next to Wangfujing Street, renowned for its silk shops. 1 E. Chang An Ave.; 800/223-1234 or 86-10/8518-1234; grand.hyatt.com; doubles from $.

Peninsula Beijing (*92.88*) Opulent hotel with Chinese-inflected design, up-to-the-minute amenities, and one of the city's finest spas. 8 Goldfish Lane; 866/382-8388 or 86-10/8516-2888; peninsula.com; doubles from $$.

Ritz-Carlton, Financial Street (*93.04*) A stylish hotel in a glass-and-steel skyscraper in the buzzy Financial District, near upscale shopping at Seasons Place. 1 Jin Cheng Fang St.; 800/241-3333 or 86-10/6601-6666; ritzcarlton.com; doubles from $$.

Shangri-La Hotel (*86.30*) Two Financial District towers offering a tranquil refuge (the grounds feature koi ponds and pavilions) from the city's vibrant urban din. 29 Zizhuyuan Rd.; 866/565-5050 or 86-10/6841-2211; shangri-la.com; doubles from $.

St. Regis (*90.67*) Alexandra Champalimaud–designed interiors (lacquered wood cabinetry; copper- and gold-hued fabrics) and exceptional service are the draw at this tony hotel. 21 Jianguomenwai Dajie; 877/787-3447 or 86-10/6460-6688; stregis.com; doubles from $$.

Westin Chaoyang (*87.46*) Three-year-old hotel in downtown's embassy district, with a soaring lobby atrium, 20 minutes by car from the airport—closer than most. 7 N. Dongsanhuan Rd.; 800/228-3000; westin.com; doubles from $$.

HONG KONG

Conrad (*88.28*) Larger-than-average guest rooms on floors 40 through 61 of the Pacific Place towers, overlooking Victoria Peak. 88 Queensway; 800/266-7237; conradhotels.com; doubles from $$$.

Four Seasons Hotel (*91.86*) Sleek, minimalist, altogether luxurious: this 399-room property is set in a tower in the International Finance Center, near the Star Ferry. 8 Finance St.; 800/332-3442 or 852/3196-8888; fourseasons.com; doubles from $$$.

InterContinental (*89.17*) Overlooking Kowloon, with restaurants by Alain Ducasse and Nobu Matsuhisa and the best Victoria Harbour views in town. 18 Salisbury Rd.; 800/327-0200; intercontinental. com; doubles from $$.

Island Shangri-La (*91.43*) The city's tallest hotel attracts financiers and shoppers thanks to its proximity to major banks and the Pacific Place Mall. Pacific Place, Supreme Court Rd.; 866/565-5050 or 852/2877-3838; shangri-la.com; doubles from $$.

Kowloon Shangri-La (*88.80*) A 688-room hotel on Kowloon's Tsim Sha Tsui East waterfront, with floor-to-ceiling bay windows in every room. 64 Mody Rd.; 866/565-5050 or 852/2721-2111; shangri-la.com; doubles from $$.

Mandarin Oriental (*92.84*) A 1960's-era mid-rise hotel, graciously updated and filled with Asian antiques, at the heart of bustling Central. 5 Connaught Rd.; 800/526-6566 or 852/2820-4202; mandarinoriental.com; doubles from $$$.

Peninsula Hong Kong (*94.11*) Ultra-luxe, colonial-style Kowloon landmark with a dazzling Philippe Starck–designed rooftop restaurant. Salisbury Rd.; 866/382-8388; peninsula.com; doubles from $$$.

SHANGHAI

Four Seasons Hotel (*89.90*) A 421-room, 37-story building—one block from Nanjing Road—with the city's grandest lobby and excellent business amenities. 500 Weihai Rd.; 800/332-3442 or 86-21/6256-8888; fourseasons.com; doubles from $$.

JW Marriott Hotel at Tomorrow Square (*87.17*) Still among the best-located of Shanghai's hotels, occupying the upper floors of a steel-and-glass skyscraper at the edge of People's Square. 399 Nanjing W. Rd.; 800/228-9290 or 86-21/5359-4969; jwmarriott.com; doubles from $$.

Pudong Shangri-La (*89.90*) In Pudong's Lujiazui financial district, this 952-room riverfront hotel includes top-notch extras (a tennis court; an Adam Tihany–designed restaurant). 33 Fu Cheng Rd.; 866/565-5050 or 86-21/6882-8888; shangri-la.com; doubles from $$.

St. Regis (*89.91*) Red-granite Pudong high-rise that mixes classic interiors with Chinese art and ceramics. 889 Dong Fang Rd.; 877/787-3447 or 86-21/5050-4567; stregis.com; doubles from $$$.

Westin Bund Center (*87.05*) Two 26-story towers with streamlined interiors (a glass staircase; beige-and-white rooms), a five-minute walk from the historic Bund. 88

Henan Central Rd.; 800/228-3000 or 86-21/6335-1888; westin.com; doubles from $$.

INDIA

AGRA

Oberoi Amarvilas (*95.94*) Moghul-themed palace mirroring the nearby Taj Mahal—all Moorish archways, patterned domes, intricate pavilions, and fountained courtyards. Taj E. Gate Rd.; 800/562-3764 or 91-562/223-1515; oberoihotels.com; doubles from $$$$.

BENGALURU (BANGALORE)

Leela Palace Kempinski (*92.27*) Opulent, domed hotel situated on a seven-acre oasis with a 14-foot waterfall, close to the city's airport and I.T. hubs. 23 Airport Rd.; 800/426-3135 or 91-80/2521-1234, kempinski.com; doubles from $$.

JAIPUR

Oberoi Rajvilas (*94.78*) Modern Rajasthani tent-and-villa retreat that combines exacting standards with the romance of a bygone era. Goner Rd.; 800/562-3764 or 91-141/268-0101; oberoihotels.com; doubles from $$$$.

Rambagh Palace (*93.60*) Former 19th-century royal hunting lodge and guesthouse on 47 manicured acres. Bhawani Singh Rd.; 866/969-1825 or 91-141/2211-919; tajhotels.com; doubles from $$$$.

JODHPUR

Umaid Bhawan Palace (*90.96*) Once the world's largest private residence; now the enormous sandstone structure with a 143-foot-high cupola is a Taj Hotel. 866/969-1825 or 91-291/251-0101; tajhotels.com; doubles from $$$$, including breakfast.

MUMBAI

The Oberoi (*88.00*) Sleek, airy, and recently renovated tower popular with business travelers, rising above the Queen's Necklace along Back Bay. Nariman Point; 800/562-3764 or 91-22/6632-5757; oberoihotels.com; doubles from $$$.

Taj Mahal Palace (*93.83*) A 1903 emblem of Raj-era Bombay, and still the city's grande dame, overlooking the Gateway of India. Apollo Bunder; 866/969-1825 or 91-22/6665-3366; tajhotels.com; doubles from $$$.

NEW DELHI

The Imperial (*90.27*) Art Deco icon, filled with potted palms and colonial antiques, steps from Connaught Place. Janpath; 800/323 7500 or 91-11/2334-1234; theimperialindia.com; doubles from $$.

The Oberoi (*86.38*) Business-friendly hotel close to Humayun's Tomb and Khan Market, with superb on-site restaurants and bars. Dr. Zakir Hussain Marg; 800/562-3764 or 91-11/2436-3030; oberoihotels.com; doubles from $$

Taj Mahal Hotel (*89.09*) An 11-story landmark in Lutyens' Delhi, near government and diplomatic offices. 1 Mansingh Rd.; 866/969-1825 or 91-11/2302-6162; tajhotels.com; doubles from $$.

Taj Palace Hotel (*89.39*) Three-wing building with a business focus, close to the airport. Sardar Patel Marg, Diplomatic Enclave; 866/969-1825 or 91-11/2611-0202; tajhotels.com; doubles from $$.

SAWAI MADHOPUR

Oberoi Vanyavilas (*97.26*) A *haveli* main lodge, 25 luxe jungle tents, and a spa next to Ranthambore National Park & Tiger Reserve.

Ranthambhore Rd.; 800/562-3764 or 91-74/6222-3999; oberoihotels.com; doubles from $$$$.

UDAIPUR

Oberoi Udaivilas (*94.71*) Opulent Mewari palace-style hotel spread across 30 acres next to Lake Pichola. Haridasji Ki Magri; 800/562-3764 or 91-294/243-3300; oberoihotels.com; doubles from $$$$.

Taj Lake Palace (*93.46*) This lavishly restored 18th-century white-marble palace is set on its own island at the center of Lake Pichola. Lake Pichola; 866/969-1825 or 91-294/242-8800; tajhotels.com; doubles from $$$$.

INDONESIA

BALI

Four Seasons Resort at Jimbaran Bay (*90.80*) 156 thatched-roof villas, all with private plunge pools, on a hillside above a secluded white-sand beach. Jimbaran; 800/332-3442 or 62-361/701-010; fourseasons.com; doubles from $$$.

The entrance courtyard at the Oberoi Vanyavilas, in Ranthambore, India.

JAPAN
KYOTO

Hyatt Regency (86.60) Traditional touches (kimono-covered headboards; *washi* paper lampshades) in the Higashiyama Shichijo district. 6-44-2 Sanjusangendo-mawari; 800/233-1234 or 81-75/541-1234; hyatt.com; doubles from $$.

TOKYO

Grand Hyatt (86.82) A tranquil 21-story hotel with 389 rooms in one of the city's premier shopping districts. 6-10-3 Roppongi; 800/233-1234 or 81-3/4333-1234; hyatt.com; doubles from $$$.

LAOS
LUANG PRABANG

La Résidence Phou Vao (87.77) French colonial–style hotel on a hill covered with frangipani on the southern edge of town. 800/237-1236 or 856-71/212-194; residencephouvao.com; doubles from $$, including breakfast.

MALAYSIA
KUALA LUMPUR

Mandarin Oriental (89.69) A 643-room retreat with floor-to-ceiling windows) next to the Petronas Twin Towers. Kuala Lumpur City Centre; 800/526-6566 or 60-3/2179-8818; mandarinoriental.com; doubles from $, including breakfast.

PHILIPPINES
BORACAY

Discovery Shores (90.35) Whitewashed buildings and a new spa on Long Beach. 800/525-4800 or 63-36/288-4500; discoveryshoresboracay.com; doubles from $$, including breakfast.

CEBU

Shangri-La's Mactan Resort & Spa (88.89) The 32-acre retreat has an impressive pool and a private white-sand beach. Punta Engano Rd., Lapu-Lapu; 866/565-5050 or 63-32/231-0288; shangri-la.com; doubles from $$, including breakfast.

MANILA

Makati Shangri-La (91.03) A 699-room hotel in the city's financial center. Ayala and Makati Aves.; 866/565-5050 or 63-2/813-8888; shangri-la.com; doubles from $$.

Peninsula Manila (90.82) Renovated in 2008, twin 11-story towers are conveniently situated near boutiques. 1226 Makati City; 866/382-8388 or 63-2/887-2888; peninsula.com; doubles from $$.

SINGAPORE

Four Seasons Hotel (94.75) The city's largest guest rooms, right in the bustling Orchard Road shopping district. 190 Orchard Blvd.; 800/332-3442 or 65/6734-1110; fourseasons.com; doubles from $$.

Fullerton Hotel (90.50) A colonnaded Neoclassical building on Marina Bay. 1 Fullerton Square; 65/6733-8388; fullertonhotel.com; doubles from $$.

Pan Pacific (87.05) On Marina Bay Harbor, 778 rooms, a relaxation deck, and a John Portman–designed atrium. 7 Raffles Blvd.; 877/324-4856 or 65/6336-8111; panpacific.com; doubles from $$.

Raffles Hotel (90.76) In cloister-like buildings, 103 high-ceilinged suites; former guests include Ava Gardner and Pablo Neruda. 1 Beach Rd.; 800/768-9009 or 65/6337-1886; raffles.com; doubles from $$$$$.

Ritz-Carlton, Millenia (86.83) Soaring tower designed by Pritzker Prize–winning architect Kevin Roche, on Marina Bay. 7 Raffles Ave.; 800/241-3333 or 65/6337-8888; ritzcarlton.com; doubles from $$$.

Shangri-La Hotel (94.32) Three wings plus 15 landscaped acres in the city's shopping hub. 22 Orange Grove Rd.; 866/565-5050 or 65/6737-3644; shangri-la.com; doubles from $$$.

THAILAND
BANGKOK

Four Seasons Hotel (90.72) Colonial charm meets Asian flair at this oasis of gardens and hand-painted silks. 155 Rajadamri Rd.; 800/332-3442 or 66-2/126-8866; fourseasons.com; doubles from $.

Grand Hyatt Erawan (87.25) Ultramodern retreat overlooking the Erawan Shrine. The 23,000-square-foot spa was designed by Tony Chi. 494 Rajadamri Rd.; 800/233-1234 or 66-2/254-1234; grand.hyatt.com; doubles from $.

Le Méridien Bangkok's sleek Bamboo Chic restaurant.

Le Méridien (89.60) The company's relaunched flagship, with tech-savvy amenities. 40/5 Surawong Rd.; 800/543-4300 or 66-2/232-8888; lemeridien.com; doubles from $$, including breakfast.

Mandarin Oriental (92.89) A 135-year-old landmark with a rich literary history on the Chao Phraya River. 48 Oriental Ave.; 800/526-6566; mandarinoriental.com; doubles from $$.

Peninsula Bangkok (95.69) An ultra-luxe hotel with 370 rooms, a three-story spa, and top dining—all at the river's edge. 333 Charoennakorn Rd.; 866/382-8388; peninsula.com; doubles from $$.

Shangri-La Hotel (88.90) An 801-room riverfront tower in the buzzing Bangrak district. 89 Soi Wat Suan Plu, New Rd.; 866/565-5050 or 66-2/236-7777; shangri-la.com; doubles from $$.

Sheraton Grande Sukhumvit, a Luxury Collection Hotel (87.27) Central city property with 420 rooms, a third-floor lagoon pool, and a top-tier concierge. 250 Sukhumvit Rd.; 800/325-3589 or 66-2/649-8888; luxurycollection.com; doubles from $.

CHIANG MAI

Four Seasons Resort (93.95) Tranquil refuge outside the city, with haute-rustic wood pavilions perched above a working rice paddy. Mae Rim-Samoeng Old Rd.; 800/332-3442 or 66-5/329-8181; fourseasons.com; doubles from $$$.

Mandarin Oriental Dhara Dhevi (93.26) A miniature Thai kingdom: 123 Lanna-inspired suites and villas on 60 acres. 51/4 Sankampaeng Rd.; 800/526-6566; mandarinoriental.com; doubles from $$$.

CHIANG SAEN

Anantara Golden Triangle Resort & Spa (90.67) On a misty mountain ridge along the Mekong, 19 thatched-roof suites. 229 Moo 1; 800/525-4800; anantara.com; doubles from $$$.

PHUKET

Amanpuri (90.60) The first entry in the Amanresorts collection and as stylish as ever: 40 tabak-wood pavilions on the Andaman Sea. Pansea Beach; 800/477-9180 or 66-7/632-4333; amanresorts.com; doubles from $$$$.

JW Marriott Resort & Spa (89.03) Secluded eco-resort and spa beside a pristine stretch of Mai Khao beach. 231 Moo 3, Mai Khao; 800/228-9290 or 66-7/633-8000; jwmarriott.com; doubles from $$.

VIETNAM

HANOI

Hilton Opera (87.53) Business-friendly hotel in Hanoi's French Quarter, blocks from Hoan Kiem Lake. 1 Le Thanh Tong St.; 800/445-8667 or 84-4/3933-0500; hilton.com; doubles from $.

Sofitel Legend Metropole (90.87) The city's grande dame. All 364 rooms include modern amenities, but those in the original wing have a traditional feel. 15 Ngo Quyen St.; 800/763-4835 or 84-4/3826-6919; sofitel.com; doubles from $$.

HO CHI MINH CITY

Caravelle Hotel (88.40) As central as it gets: two Art Deco buildings with 335 rooms on trendy Lam Son Square. 19 Lam Son Square, District 1; 800/223-5652 or 84-8/3823-4999; caravellehotel.com; doubles from $$.

Park Hyatt Saigon (87.72) Colonial-style contemporary on the main square, with two good restaurants and the city's only nonsmoking bar. 2 Lam Son Square, District 1; 877/875-4658 or 84-8/3824-1234; park.hyatt.com; doubles from $$.

Australia, New Zealand, & the South Pacific

AUSTRALIA

GREAT BARRIER REEF

Hayman (90.00) Luxurious hotel, on a private island in the Coral Sea, that just added eight new suites. Hayman Island; 800/223-6800 or 61-7/4940-1838; hayman.com.au; doubles from $$$, including breakfast.

MELBOURNE

The Langham (91.50) Langham's first outpost; now featuring marble bathrooms and Waterford crystal chandeliers—just blocks from the Royal Botanic Garden. 1 Southgate Ave.; 800/588-9141 or 61-3/8696-8888; langhamhotels.com; doubles from $$.

Park Hyatt (87.06) Art Deco gem overlooking St. Patrick's Cathedral and Fitzroy Gardens, with superb service. 1 Parliament Square; 877/875-4658 or 61-3/9224-1234; park.hyatt.com; doubles from $$.

SYDNEY

Park Hyatt (87.68) It's all about location at this 155-room harborside hotel, which overlooks the Opera House and is a five-minute stroll from downtown. 7 Hickson Rd.; 877/875-4658 or 61-2/9256-1234; park.hyatt.com; doubles from $$$.

Shangri-La Hotel (86.89) Set in the Rocks, a historic neighborhood anchored by an outdoor market and the Contemporary Museum of Art, and offering Sydney's largest rooms. 176 Cumberland St.; 866/565-5050; shangri-la.com; doubles from $$.

FRENCH POLYNESIA

BORA-BORA

InterContinental Resort & Thalasso Spa (89.87) The ultimate beachgoer's fantasy: 80 thatch-roofed overwater villas and a 43,056-square-foot spa above an azure lagoon. Motu Piti Auau; 800/327-0200 or 689/60-76-00; ichotelsgroup.com; doubles from $$$$$.

NEW ZEALAND

AUCKLAND

Hilton (86.71) Light-filled showstopper (white-on-white rooms; floor-to-ceiling windows) on a pier near Queen Street. 147 Quay St.; 800/445-8667 or 64-9/978-2000; hilton.com; doubles from $$$.

Pullman (formerly Hyatt Regency) (86.20) A 347-room high-rise hotel with views of Auckland Harbour. Corner of Princes St. and Waterloo Quadrant; 800/515-5679 or 64-9/353-1000; pullmanauckland.co.nz; doubles from $.

CHRISTCHURCH

The George (88.13) The region's leading boutique hotel, with a 1-to-1 staff-to-guest ratio. 50 Park Terrace; 800/525-4800 or 64-3/379-4560; thegeorge.com; doubles from $$.

TAUPO

Huka Lodge (91.25) The sine qua non of North Island lodges, thanks to a roster of activities and an idyllic Lake Taupo setting. 271 Huka Falls Rd.; 800/223-6800 or 64-7/378-5791; hukaretreats.com; doubles from $$$$$, including breakfast and dinner. ✚

Alila Villas Uluwatu's pool and outdoor cabanas, in Bali, Indonesia.

trips directory

A Terry Richardson
photograph and Jean Prouvé
bench at Hôtel Ermitage, in
St.-Tropez, France.

index

A dining pavilion at Javvu restaurant, in Shangri-La's Villingili Resort & Spa, in the Maldives.

contributors

Richard Alleman
Barbara Ascher
Tom Austin
Luke Barr
Thomas Beller
Sylvie Bigar
Dominique Browning
Alice Bruneau
Andrew Burke
Paul Chai
Jennifer Chen
Lisa Cheng
Matt Chesterton
Mark Chestnut
Mark Chipperfield
Christine Ciarmello
Anthony Dennis
Roberto Gutiérrez Durán
Irene Edwards
Mark Ellwood
Kristina Ensminger

Jennifer Flowers
Janet Forman
Meghann Foye
Eleni Gage
Charles Gandee
Jane Garmey
Alice Gordon
Jaime Gross
Serra Gurcay
Farhad Heydari
Catesby Holmes
Tina Isaac
Amin Jaffer
James Jung
Laurie Kahle
David Kaufman
Melik Kaylan
Josh Krist
Chris Kucway
Kelly Lack
Peter Jon Lindberg

Mimi Lombardo
Alexandra Marshall
Steve Meacham
Mario R. Mercado
Carolina A. Miranda
Clark Mitchell
Shane Mitchell
Ian Mount
Suzanne Mozes
Nancy Novogrod
Mark Orwoll
Kathryn O'Shea-Evans
Benedetta Pignatelli
Helen Pipins
Sandra Ramani
Dorkys Ramos
Rodrigo Pérez Rembao
Katerina Roberts
Sophy Roberts
Sean Rocha
Adam Sachs

Karen Schaler
Bruce Schoenfeld
Jim Shi
Maria Shollenbarger
Gary Shteyngart
Samai Singh
Sarah Beth Spagnolo
Bree Sposato
Tara Stevens
Sarah Storms
Rima Suqi
Leisa Tyler
Laura Teusink
Guy Trebay
Meeghan Truelove
Daniela Vaca
Anya von Bremzen
Valerie Waterhouse
Sally Webb
Pamela Young

Vintage postcards at Hotel Boca Chica Acapulco, in Mexico.

photographers

A magazine of modern global culture, *Travel + Leisure* examines the places, ideas, and
trends that define the way we travel now. T+L inspires readers to explore
the world, equipping them with expert advice and a better understanding of the endless
possibilities of travel. Delivering clear, comprehensive service journalism, intelligent
writing, and evocative photography, T+L is the authority for today's traveler.
Visit us at TravelandLeisure.com.